To Gerry E Bowland

Best wishes
Betty K Cooper

# SPEAK WITH POWER

Six Steps
And
Eight Keys
For
Speaking Success

# Betty K. Cooper

## Canadian Cataloguing in Publication Data

### Cooper, Betty K,

Speak with power:
Six steps and eight keys for speaking success

### ISBN 0-9699163-0-2

1.  Speaking     2.  Public Speaking
3.  Presentations     4.  Business Communications
I.  Pow!-R Press.   II.  Title

### Published by:
Pow!-R Publications
336 - 40 Street, S.W.
Calgary, Alberta   T3C 1V8

### Design and computer generated graphics
### by Debi Whistlecraft

### Original hand drawn graphics and cartoons
### by Adam Kolody

### Front cover and Jacket Design
### by Debi Whistlecraft

### Printed in Canada by:
Classic Printing Service Ltd.
Vancouver, B.C.

Published in 1994

First Edition

**This book is dedicated to my three,
dearly loved grandchildren,
Timothy, Nicola, and Jonathan.**

They are just beginning their travels
down the speaking highway.
When they are old enough to read
I hope my words will help them too.

# ACKNOWLEDGEMENTS

I find this part of my book the most difficult to write. How to zero in on those special people who helped me along the way. There are too many to name.

First I must thank the thousands of people I have worked with in my many years as a speech coach, consultant, speaker, television and radio broadcaster and producer. As we worked together to make you confident speakers I have been able to develop new ways to help this happen. Many of them are in this book.

My thanks to my first speech arts teacher and mentor, Edith Matthison. Her guidance and encouragement shaped my professional life. And to Leona Paterson, my dear friend and colleague who encouraged me to continue learning and experimenting as I worked with the business community to help clients speak with confidence. To Carol Blythe, former Co-ordinator of Continuing Education programs, Calgary Board of Education. She enthusiastically endorsed my idea to design a speaking course at a time when 'public speaking' courses were not available.

Although I have been a writer most of my adult life through commentaries, documentaries, and the numerous radio and television scripts I have produced, at times it was difficult to share my speaking concepts on paper. My family will agree - I am a talker! Fortunately they are too. Without their vocal encouragement I know I would have stopped short of my goal.

To my husband Cedric, who has been my most ardent supporter in my professional life and in our marriage, thank you. To my three sons Bill, Terry and Bob who singly, and in unison, have encouraged and prodded as needed to "finish your book"! And, who are positive walking examples of the effective speaking techniques I teach. Their enthusiasm has

i

always been shared by their partners, Alicia, Elizabeth and Averie. My thanks to you all.

Also thanks to my brother Douglas Ramsay and his wife Leone for their support. And lastly, to my late mother who always believed in me.

At the top of my list in the actual production of this book is Debi Whistlecraft. First, for immediately supporting my concept and then for applying her tremendous creative talents to every aspect of its creation. Encouraging, prompting, digging in her heels. Whatever it took to help me keep focused.

To my friends in the National Speakers Association who read and shared their ideas. To Mary Biner for helping me at the editing stage. To Laura Smith, Pamela Hat, Michelle Mayall, Joe Killi, and Bryce Medd for their special contributions. And to all my other clients and friends who contributed so generously of their time, experience and knowledge in bringing this book together.

# TABLE OF CONTENTS

# FORWARD

President, Walters International Speakers Bureau,
Glendora, Calif.

**BETTY K. COOPER** is one of the most effective and talented speaking coaches in North America. Not only is she a marvelous speech writer, but she is also a top communication professional. Betty trains many executives in platform skills, and in the ability to portray a masterful business image through their words and voice tones.

Her background as announcer, actor, talk show host, radio commentator, college drama and speech teacher, give her a treasure chest of talents which she uses with charm and ability to help others perform. From the first moment you meet her in person, or in the words of this book, you will feel her warmth and creativity.

This book is much needed by everyone who communicates one-to-one, and who makes presentations to boards of directors, potential clients, and large or small audiences. The quality of the voice itself and how to develop it is one of Betty's most famous areas of expertise.

As publisher/editor of Sharing Ideas newsmagazine for professional speakers, I am an avid reader about leaders who are remembered for their voices, as well as their words.

Such a man was ***Lord Kitchener***, who won three major wars for the British: Egypt, South Africa, and India. They said of Lord Kitchener that he knew at all times where every man and every piece of ordinance under his command was located. And, when he spoke, he used the ***"Voice of Command"***. No matter what his size or looks, his voice had the iron ring of the leader. Today's business leaders need to develop this powerful executive tool.

It is said, "When the student is ready, the teacher appears." You hold in your hand this great book. It contains the help of a mighty voice, speech and drama coach, **BETTY K. COOPER.** If you are ready to develop the *"Voice of Command"* your teacher is here.

"As a vessel is known by the sound,
whether it be cracked or not,
so people are proved by their speeches
whether they are wise or foolish."

**Demosthenes**

# INTRODUCTION

**Sheridan once said of a speech,**

"It contained a great deal
both of what was new and what was true.
The problem was that
what was new was not true
and what was true was not new."

As the quotes on the previous page state, communicating can have its problems.

# BASIC ORAL COMMUNICATION PROBLEMS

- Speaker appears nervous
- Speaker doesn't seem to have any energy
- Speaker does not connect with audience in first twenty words
- Speaker forgets to keep eye contact with audience
- Speaker's voice is difficult to listen to - too high, too low, too fast, too slow.
- Speaker's information is interesting but presentation is boring.
- Speaker does not use effective vocal variety (pace, pitch, pauses, inflection, volume, emphasis, modulation, projection)
- Speaker's language is not suited to listener or occasion.
- Speaker's body language and text do not go together. Face lacks expression. Body is tense or gestures inappropriate.
- Speaker does not involve audience emotionally.
- Speaker is reading instead of sharing from script.

On the following pages you will learn how to effectively communicate and deal with these problems and thereby **POW ! - R Speak** for **Business Success.**

> "It ain't what you say,
> it's the way that you say it
> that gets results!"

**W**ith the words of that old song, I have introduced thousands of people to their true voices through courses, seminars, workshops,and talks!

Like the many other business people, broadcasters, and actors I have worked with, you will learn the truth of that old song.

There is a murmured *"yes"* when I ask workshop participants if they've heard their voices on tape. When I "drop the other shoe" and ask if they like the sound, a moan goes up! Not many really like the voice they hear.

- **Like it or not, the voice you hear on a tape recorder is the voice others hear.**

This is the age of Voice Mail; Answering Machines; Business by telephone; Presentations to get people to buy your ideas or products.

- **You cannot afford to speak in a manner even you don't like!**

**POW ! - R Speaking** will give you the critical edge you need. You'll speak in a way that invites positive listening and reaction. On the practical side **POW ! - R Speaking** can help you acquire the extra you need to move ahead in your world.

3

This book is designed to help you take charge of your voice and your future! Wishing won't make it so. Working with this book will. It will move you from *'wishing and wanting'* to *'learning and doing'*!

● **Studies show
audiences gain their impression of you
NOT by what you say
BUT how you say it.**

● **Less than ten percent of your impact
is from the words themselves.**

To prove this point, I often start a workshop by having participants talk in **NUMBERS**. I partner them up. They then have to carry on a conversation using in turn only the words *"one-two-three-four-five"* Try it. It works even if you talk to yourself! You'll discover you really talk in stereo.

## Example:

| | |
|---|---|
| **Partner 1** | (thinks:"Why did you say THAT?")<br>SAYS: "One-two-three-four-FiiiiiVE?" |
| **Partner 2** | (thinks: "WHY did I say what?")<br>SAYS :"ONE-two-three-four-five?"<br>And so on... |

As you say the words you think of a comment or suggestion. This is your hidden message. You have a *"hidden message"* you say to yourself before you speak. What comes out of your mouth is the result of this inner voice. The **WHY** you are saying what you say in a particular way.

## That is what this book is all about.

- It will help you **"Put your best voice forward"**.

- You will learn how your voice works and how to make it work for you.

- With this book as your guide you will embark on a new and exciting communications journey; a sharing of ideas not simply talking.

- You'll learn to use the Eight CooperKeys to release your vocal power.

- You'll climb the Six Steps to Speaking Success.

- It will help you prepare formal or informal presentations

- You will be better able to organize your ideas so people will get your message easily

- It shows you how to harness your **Voice Power** and how to **POW ! - R Talk.**

# How important is POW ! - R Speaking?

I was working with a young woman lawyer. One of her major problems was getting the judge to listen to her.

"Even when I introduce myself he doesn't seem to hear me!" she remarked.

We worked on her phrasing, pausing, projection and inflection at our first session.

The next time she came full of confidence and smiles. She had put her new speaking tools to work and the judge really listened!

Not only that, a colleague was so impressed he asked her, "How did you get your ideas across so clearly today?"

From the other side of the bench, a participant of the first course I ever taught in **POW ! - R Speaking** is now a judge! He used the Keys and Steps you will find here to forge a successful law career. Morever, before becoming a judge he was active in municipal politics and renowned for his speaking power.

Another example showing the importance of effective *Power Speaking* in relationship to getting your message across came when I was a daily commentator for CBC Radio. I had given one of my more contraversial comments one morning and a listener phoned in to talk about it. She disagreed with my stand and this is what she said.

"I don't think it's fair," she said. "When you say something, you say it in such a positive manner everyone believes you!"

I replied - with true appreciation, "Thank you!! You've made my day and perhaps the rest of my life. That is just what I want to do!"

It is what we **ALL** want to do, isn't it!

- **Being able to use your voice effectively can literally change your life.**

Let me share a special moment with you. It was the first night of a short course I was giving on *'Speaking with Confidence'*. During the first hour we'd learned about my eight keys and six steps. We'd done some short exercises to demonstrate how they worked. Then it was time for the class to talk. The sixth person to get up to speak was a young woman about twenty-five.

Speaking in a very "gravelly" voice, she said: "I was in a very bad car accident about two years ago. I damaged my throat and have been in therapy for over six months. My therapist told me to take this course as she thought it would help me become more confident while having to talk this way. Well, let me tell you. I've learned more about how to use my voice in this past hour than I learned in the past six months."

**But that isn't the end.** At the next class - four days later - she got up to speak. Only a trace of the 'gravel' was there - at the beginning of a few phrases! By the end of the four sessions she had mastered the lesson of power placement! Her voice was **OK**!

She had learned to speak from her power centre **through** her throat not pushing **with** her throat. This is a very important point in power speaking.

This book isn't for people who need therapy. I shared this girl's story with you to underscore what this book **IS** about.

● **It is about finding your voice and making it work for you.**

If *"finding your POW ! - R CENTRE"* can help someone with a damaged set of pipes - think how effective you will be when you harness all *Eight CooperKeys* to effective speaking!

● **Remember this - you have the voice you want. It's inside you.**

● **This book gives you the Steps and the Keys to unlock your voice.**

● **It then moves you to practical ways to organize what you say.**

From Desire to Platform Polish there are practical ideas you will start to use right away. People will listen when you talk.

They will hear a pleasing voice, speaking with a focus that makes it easy for people to listen and to respond positively.

In this book you'll find the six steps and eight keys needed to make you a better, more effective speaker. Your presentations will be focused and motivating. In your business as well as your personal life you will be able to speak so that people listen and buy into your ideas.

Start now to unlock the doors and climb six steps to speaking success. You will enjoy the journey.

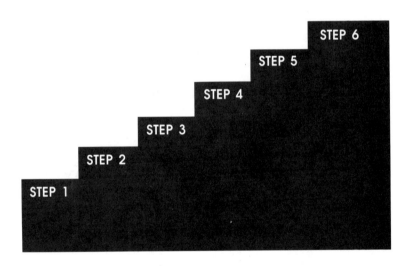

**TO START**

How to turn stonewalls
into stepping stones
for power speaking success

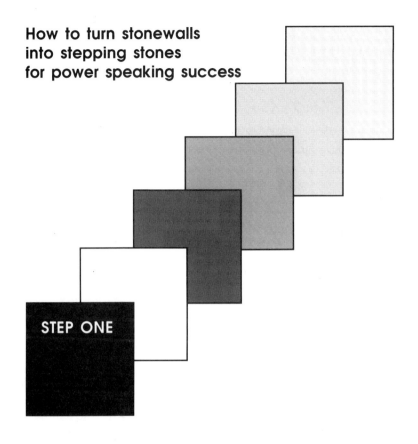

STEP ONE

# THE
# EIGHT KEYS
# TO
# POW ! - R
# SPEAKING

**YOU HAVE THE VOICE.** What you need to do is *"Let it out!"*. The eight CooperKeys will unlock your speaking power.

The next eight chapters give you the tools you need to take this first **GIANT** step. Here is a *Road Map* to help you get ready for the trip.

KEY NO. 1

## DESIRE

You already have this key! You're reading this page. In this book you will learn how to capitalize on your good intentions - your dream for success.

It isn't enough to dream. Dreams *can* be a preview of your future success. To make dreams a reality you need to dress them in working clothes.

KEY NO. 2

## DEVELOP YOUR POW ! - R BASE

You must learn to control your breath from your **POW ! - R Centre.** Some people call it "belly breathing". What you need to do is fill the lower lungs with air and control the exhaling from that power centre. That is where you have flexibility. You can push your diaphragm down. You can lift your ribs. You can work with the band of abdominal muscles circling the waist.

Only then can you take control of the most important key on your Speech Key chain - your Breath. how to breathe effectively for speaking support and control.

You *must* learn to *Breathe for Success.* A Rolls Royce is not going to take you far without gas. And you won't get a smooth ride unless the engine is tuned up.

10

Your voice is just like a car. This key shows you how to keep the breath *"topped up"*. How to control the outgoing breath for positive power!

**KEY NO. 3**

## MATCH YOUR VOICE TO YOUR MESSAGE

You must know how to make your voice amplify your personality and your message. If you have a tendency to be Monotone Mike or Janey-one-note or any of the other labels a lazy voice gives you - you need to work with this key.

You have at least a dozen pitches you can use with ease. If you are like most speakers, you are using one or two! You can learn to pattern the speaking part of your brain. Automatically use all the pitches you need as you express a new idea.

**KEY NO. 4**

## POW ! - R TALKING

The second most important key. This key enables you to help listeners **REALLY** understand your message. I call this key the key to understanding!

You have to learn to apply interpretation tools. **PITCH - PACE - PAUSE - PROJECTION.** These are the major movers. We speak in ideas not words. Each new idea has to be vocally separated.

In writing you can use commas, periods, sentences, paragraphs, capital letters and so on. In speech you do all this critical interpretation with your voice.

And remember...when you are speaking people are listening to you with half an ear - if that! Your vocal ability to orchestrate your message will be the difference between making or not making your point.

11

- **The first four keys focused on you - the speaker. The next four look the other way - at your listener.**

KEY NO. 5

## P.R.E.P. FOR SUCCESS

You have to structure your message to make this key open yet another door to speaking success. Strong structures start with a strong foundation.

Your foundation must be *"What do I want my listener to do/know when I finish talking?"* Specifically!

Too many people start with *"What do I want to say?"* Unless you say it in terms of action you'll end up with non-committed listeners.

KEY NO. 6

## DEVELOP "AA" AUDIENCE APPRECIATION

When you talk from a "What do I want to say?" position you ignore the reason you are speaking. Your listener. Your audience. You want to share ideas with someone. You must know your audience. Only then will you know how to orchestrate your message specifically for those ears. You will share with - not speak at!

KEY NO. 7

## UNDERSTAND THE 'EYE' & 'I' NEEDS

You cannot communicate if you do not look at the person or people you are talking to! You cannot look at your script or notes while you are speaking. You must learn to look; lift ideas; then share them looking at those you are talking to!

12

### "Mouth open = eyes up!"

This is half of this key. The other half - *think in terms of the audience*. The password to your speaking success is not **"I"** but **"YOU"**. You will learn to orchestrate your message to do this effectively.

**KEY NO. 8**

## APPLY "P & P" - PRACTICE AND PATIENCE

You can be as good a speaker as you want to be. It is up to you.

The steps and Keys are here...the door won't open if you don't turn the key! Practice the techniques and they become automatic - just like driving skills.

You don't learn to play a piano by leaning against it! You cannot improve your speaking skills by thinking about them!

Work carefully with each key to successfully take the first giant step to speaking with confidence. Understanding and using these keys will make all the other steps so much easier.

Trying to harness your potential speaking power *without* using these keys will make the other steps as difficult as walking in gumbo mud!

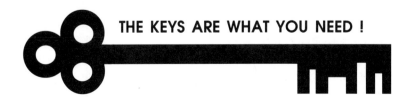

**THE KEYS ARE WHAT YOU NEED !**

## COMMUNICATIONS SKILLS CHECK LIST

## HOW GOOD A COMMUNICATOR ARE YOU?

Look at this list. *Note areas* where you feel you need improvement. As you work through the **KEYS** check back. Revise as you acquire and learn to use the communicating tools you need.

|  | Yes | No | Need Work |
|---|---|---|---|
| • I feel I can control my nerves when talking to a small or large group |  |  |  |
| • My posture always reflects a positive image |  |  |  |
| • I adapt my approach to suit audience |  |  |  |
| • I'm happy about the way I sound when I speak |  |  |  |
| • I'm enthusiastic about talking to a group |  |  |  |
| • I find it fairly easy to collect my thoughts and responses in impromptu situations |  |  |  |
| • People find me easy to listen to |  |  |  |
| • I usually have a positive response to my suggestions and presentations |  |  |  |

| | | | |
|---|---|---|---|
| • I always analyze my audience | | | |
| • I know how to organize my ideas for maximum impact | | | |
| • I know how to keep good eye contact even when using complete script | | | |
| • I use supporting evidence for each point I make | | | |
| • I understand the importance of the positive listening process. I use it when listening to others. | | | |
| • I know how to orchestrate my voice for maximum effect | | | |
| • I adapt my vocabulary to fit the audience; use correct grammar | | | |

**NOTES:**

_____

_____

_____

_____

_____

Use the rest of this space to note other speaking problems you want to correct. If it concerns what you say or how you say it - you will find what you need as you work with the material in this book..

Just remember. You can be as good a speaker as you want to be. You will find the tools you need here. The rest is up to you. How important is it to be an effective communicator? You won't improve by simply reading. You must work with the material here. The more you work the more quickly you will become the speaker you **CAN** be.

## Cooper Communicating Tool

**"Twenty minutes a day
and
you are on your way!"**

KEY NO. 1

**The Double "D"
Desire and Determination**

# DESIRE

The Greeks had a word for it!
Or rather, *one Greek, Helvetius*,
had several words
to say about motivation.

"A person without desire has within no
principle of action nor motive to act!"

You won't improve your ability to speak with power by passively reading this book - or any other book! You will improve quickly and dramatically as you learn to use the **Cooper Communications Tools: Your Six Steps and Eight Keys** to *"Speaking with Confidence for Success"*.

## ● You will know HOW TO BECOME an effective speaker.

You will have the tools to become as good a speaker as you want to be! I guarantee it. But - as Shakespeare says, "Ah, There's the rub!"

If you have taken lessons or trained in any sport you know practice is part of the package. You develop a strong team if you practice between games. You can play a concerto only if you have practised the scales. The basics must become automatic signals from your brain. *POW ! - R Speakering* requires the same discipline.

Fortunately, it is easy to work with your voice; easier than practicing the piano or running around on a football field! You always have your instrument with you; your voice. Use the time when you are caught in a traffic jam, having a shower, walking or jogging, or just sitting to develop your vocal effectiveness.

Twenty minutes a day and you are on your way to becoming the speaker you want to be. For the next four weeks try spending as much time each day on your voice as you do shaving or putting on *"your face"*. You will be amazed how quickly you develop speaking skills. Remember:

---

- Good speakers are NOT born.

- Good speakers are not satisfied with just getting to be average.

- Good speakers work continually to stay that way.

---

Being able to share ideas effectively can put thousands of dollars into your pocket. It can help you get that raise; make that sale; get that job; reach that special goal.

Research suggests 7% of your message gets to your listener by WHAT you say; the other 93% reaches your target by the **WAY YOU SAY IT THROUGH YOUR VOICE AND YOUR NON-VERBAL MESSAGES.**

It isn't enough to know what you want to say.

- **You have to learn to say it so people buy into your ideas!!**

To use this First Key effectively, couple your desire with a promise to yourself. *Work with your voice DAILY so it can work for you automatically.*

# DEVELOP A DAILY
# WARMUP ROUTINE

Because we **LEARN** to speak, you can program your brain to be *'at the ready'* whenever you open your mouth.

Any vocal warmup should have five steps:

1. **Relaxation**
   Body tension immediately transfers to your voice.

2. **Breathing exercises**
   You must learn to control your PowerBase.

3. **Resonating exercises**
   This gives you your full strong sound. Work on full vowel tones for colourful expression.

4. **Articulation exercises**
   Tongue twisters are an example. Your tongue moves over two hundred times every minute you speak. You must make sure your articulation organs are flexible and controlled.

5. **Apply the warm-up to speaking or reading aloud**
   Read a "letter to the editor" from your local newspaper. If you can't think of anything else - use nursery rhymes! There are some at the end of this chapter.

# HERE'S A STANDARD VOCAL WARM-UP ROUTINE

## 1.   Relaxation

**(a)**   *"Rag Doll"* stand with your feet comfortably apart; stretch arms overhead, reaching for ceiling; count silently to three, then drop over from the waist (as if you were a puppet on a string and the string has been cut); hang there with head and arms able to move limply without tension.

Start coming up again, very slowly, unfolding from the bottom of the spine to keep you relaxed, taking in a breath as you do this until you are stretching again.

Repeat, releasing air as your trunk falls forward.

**(b)**   *Yawn*, inhaling deeply and stretching the jaw as wide open as possible. Vocalize as you exhale, by saying "aaaaaaaah"!

## 2.   Breath Control and Support

**(a)**   As you count silently, do the following:

| Breath In | Hold | Breathe Out |
|-----------|------|-------------|
| 1,2,3, | 1 - 2 - 3 | 1,2,3 |
| 1,2,3, | 1 - 2 - 3 | 1,2,3,4,5, |

Continue to "9". All breath should be expelled each time.

**(b)**   *Inhale and count* from 1 to 10, from 1 to 20, from 1 to 30. Do not waste breath on voiceless consonants.

## 3. Resonance

Standing erect and relaxed, take in a breath and hum as you exhale. Try to keep the sound steady in volume and projection.

Say the following, increasing each time:

- MAW - MAY - MEE - MOH - MOO
  MAW-MAW ;MAY-MAY ;MEE-MEE ;
  MOH-MOH; MOO-MOO, etc.
  MAW-MAW-MAW; MAY-MAY-MAY;
  MEE-MEE-MEE; etc

Try to reach 5 times for each sound. Use one breath for each line.

## 4. Articulation

- Lah, lay, lee, loh, loo (repeat three times)

- Lily Lucy Lily Lucy Let Lily Lucy Let Lily Lucy Let Lily Lucy Live Later Lily Lily Lily Lily Lily Lily Lily Lily Lily Let Lily Lucy Lucy Let Lily Let Lucy Lily(5 times).

- Peggy Babcock, Peggy Babcock, Peggy Babcock

- Shirley is selling her shop at the seashore.

- Reds rule. Blue rules. (repeat three times)

- Gig whip. Gig whip. Gig whip

## 5.  Application

Here is an excerpt from Hamlet's advice to the Players, by Shakespeare, to get you started (reading aloud or speaking).

● *Speak the speech, I pray you, as I pronounced it to you, trippingly on the tongue: but if you mouth it, as many of your players do, I had as lief the town-crier spoke my lines. Nor do not saw the air too much with your hand, thus, but use all gently; for in the very torrent, tempest, and, as I may say, the whirlwind of passion, you must acquire and beget a temperance that may give it smoothness.*

## Note:

When you read the excerpt above and the nursery rhymes on the follow page try to think of them as **'real'** stories.

Put real energy into them. Use them to practice building a message to the final line.

● **It is important to see the picture before you say it.**

## SOME NURSERY RHYMES

- Old Mother Hubbard went to the
  cupboard,
  To get her poor dog a bone.
  But when she got there,
  The cupboard was bare,
  And so the poor doggie had none.

- Ladybird, ladybird fly away home.
  Your house is on fire,
  And your children alone!

# MORE NURSERY RHYMES

- There was a little girl and she had a little curl,
  Right in the middle of her forehead.
  When she was good
  She was very, very good
  But when she was bad she was horrid.

- Jack Spratt could eat no fat.
  His wife could eat no lean.
  And so between the two of them
  They licked the platter clean.

- Three blind mice.
  Three blind mice.
  See how they run. See how they run.
  They all ran after the farmer's wife,
  Who cut off their tails with a carving knife,
  Did ever you see such a sight in your life
  As three blind mice.

- A dillar, a dollar,
  A ten o'clock scholar.
  What makes you come so soon?
  You used to come at ten o'clock,
  And now you come at noon.

- Tom, Tom, the Piper's son,
  Stole a pig and away he ran.
  The pig was eat,
  Tom was beat,
  And Tom went crying down the street.

This may seem silly to you but everything has a purpose. If you can read these nursery rhymes with feeling and interest, think what you can do to something of real value and importance to you and your audience.

**KEY NO. 2**

**Breathe for power
not just for life**

# DEVELOP
# YOUR
# POW ! - R BASE

"You can put your mind into your speech;
You can put your heart into your speech;
But, if you don't put your diaphragm into it,
Your speech will have no power!"

- **POW ! - R Breathing** is what speaking is all about.
- **POW ! - R Breathing** gives colour to your talk.
- **POW ! - R Breathing** projects your voice easily.

You speak to share. You want someone to hear you - listen to you - buy into your ideas. If you have no inner physical power to match your ideas you might "just as well save your breath to cool your porridge" as my mother used to say!

My experience working with speakers at every level of performance has convinced me a good voice is just a breath away!

You may have to change your thinking about the way you breathe to speak. *There are differences between breathing to live and breathing to POW ! - R Talk.*

| BREATHING TO LIVE | BREATHING FOR SPEECH |
|---|---|
| Rhythm is constant | No fixed or regular rhythm Depends upon what is said |
| Noticeable pause between exhaling and inhaling | Breath taken in quickly - out slowly in control |
| Inhale as you need to replenish | You "top up" breath when you pause between spoken phrases |

To speak effectively you must first build your power base. Develop control of the diaphragm. Strengthen the abdominal muscles you need to help push the air out with force.

Think of a quiet pond. If you drop a pebble into it from a height of three feet, you'll make little ripples. Throw it hard from the same height and you'll have much bigger waves.

*POW ! - R Talking* works the same way. A strong push of breath power will make the vocal cords vibrate with more power. The sound impulses are amplified and resounded with more power. The sound is emitted with more power. It is fuller. It carries further without vocal strain.

*POW ! - R Breathing* doesn't mean taking in huge breaths. It doesn't mean using a great deal of breath when you speak. Quite the contrary. **CONTROLLING** your breath is the first step in managing your voice. You learn to expel your breath with controlled power.

**POW ! - R BREATHING IS THE KEY** to a controlled, effective voice. For that reason it is important to take the time to really understand how it works - for you.

● **The proper method is called Diaphragmatic-Intercostal Breathing**

a long name, but a simple process. Your lungs are pear- shaped. It makes sense to fill them to the bottom. It is the natural way; watch a baby breathing.

The breath is controlled by:

| | |
|---|---|
| **a)** | The diaphragm |
| **b)** | The abdominal muscles circling the waist |
| **c)** | The intercostal muscles that raise and lower your ribs |

On the next page look at the diagram of the lungs when they are relaxed (most of the breath expelled). Now look at the lungs in the expanded position. The greatest expansion is in the lower part of the lungs.

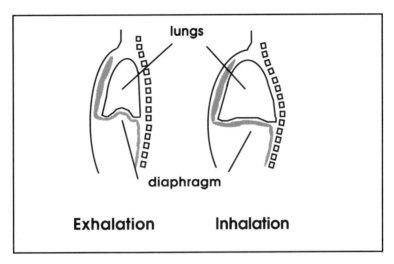

lungs

diaphragm

**Exhalation**　　　**Inhalation**

As you know the diaphragm is a large, mushroom shaped muscle attached to the bottom of the rib cage on it's outer edge. When you take in a breath the diaphragm flattens and the rib cage lifts.

By controlling the diaphragm you control the amount of air used to initiate sound and to power that sound.

## Try this:

- Take in a breath. Notice how your chest rises and the lower ribs lift outwards and upwards?

- Rest your hands on the sides of your lower rib cage and breath in. You'll feel your ribs moving up and out like a bellows.

Your breath power is centred around the lower part of your lungs. The upper parts are encased in muscle and inflexible ribs.

You cannot breathe effectively by raising your shoulders when you take in a deep breath. You can only do this by flattening your diaphragm and raising your ribs.

## Try this:

Place the palms of your hands on your stomach (just above your navel) middle fingers touching, the thumbs resting on the space where the ribs start to fan out. **TAKE A BREATH.** Feel how your hands are raised up and out as the diaphragm flattens.

## Several ways to find your POW ! - R Centre:

- Sit on chair - like a double "L". Press palm of hand three  inches above naval. Stand up. Sit down. Feel the muscles under the hand tighten.

- Stand and face a wall - place one leg in front of the other in a"fencing" position. Place palms of hands on wall (make sure you are standing far enough away so your hands take the weight of your body) **TRY TO PUSH THE WALL OVER!** Feel tension in those centre muscles.

- Clench one hand as if holding a large balloon. Place against mouth. Take a deep breath. Then blow into a softly clenched fist as though trying to blow up a large balloon in one breath.

- Say **"pull"** as you try to haul an imaginary bucket out of a well.

- Say **"push"** as you try to push an imaginary desk across a room.

- Raise your arms over your head as you take in a breath. Expel the breath quickly  as you say **"AAAAH"**. At the same time lower you arms - first straight down - then  bringing your hands together in front of your navel as you push the last ounce of breath out with force. Rather like Karate people do.

31

Now you have found your *"POW ! R Centre"* use it to help you gain vocal projection without strain and unnecessary volume.

- Place your hands lightly on your "**centre**" This is the space between your navel and the bottom of your breast bone. Rest one palm on the back of the other.

- Take in a good breath and count aloud to five. As you say "**five**" push your hands firmly inwards and upwards. Your voice will suddenly be stronger and louder. That's **POW ! - R Centring.**

## Cooper Communicating Tool

- **Middle or centre breathing, using the diaphragm, lets you SPEAK THROUGH THE THROAT NOT WITH IT!**

You can talk all day; cheer your team all night and never strain your vocal cords! When you talk from your power base you will never suffer from a strained voice or throat.

When you *"push"* the voice from the upper chest you will tighten the muscles all around your throat. The result: a strained voice and a shouting sound . If you've ever ended up with a sore throat from *"shouting"* or talking too long your voice is *"Off-centre"*. Try this exercise:

- Get a small book. Lie on your back on the floor. Place the book on your abdomen - just above your navel.

- Take in a deep breath concentrating on the book. Try to raise it as you take in a breath. Lower it as your let the breath out.

- Expel the air in different ways: Blow out through rounded lips; say "AH", or "EE"; let it out with controlled "HAW-HAW-HAW etc."

You don't have to take huge, deep breaths as you *"keep your power supply filled"*.

When you **POW ! - R TALK**, you do not use a lot of breath. Quite the contrary. Too many people take in a deep breath - then talk until all that supply is gone. It may leave you in the middle of a very important piece of information you are sharing. It may cause you to fade away at the end of phrases.

To develop and utilize *Controlled Breath Power* to *POW ! - R TALK* you must learn to:

- Sip in breath to **"top-up"** at suitable pausing opportunities.

- Control outgoing breath so only necessary breath is used.

- Push that air from the diaphragm with force.

With your breath controlled **YOU** decide the **WAY** you speak as well as **WHAT** you say!

Powerful voices move nations! Not by being **LOUD**, but by being **CONTROLLED**. Great singers know this. Musicians who play wind instruments know this.

I remember reading a comment by Frank Sinatra. He was asked how he learned to control and bend his voice so well. He replied that it was from watching the way Tommy Dorsey managed his breath support while playing the trombone.

*The secret to powerful talking -* keep those lungs comfortably filled - not bursting with uncontrollable power.

At the end of each idea you pause, sip in a little breath if you need it, then continue speaking. You don't have to breathe in at every pause. You do use a pause to replenish.

33

# RELAXATION

Did you ever try to shoot a ball through a basket? Hit a golf ball? Dive or swim? If so, you already know how important it is to relax and concentrate.

To breathe with ease and to speak with ease you must also learn to **RELAX**. Tight muscles will affect your voice. *Power Talk* starts first with relaxation and concentration.

**TRAIN YOURSELF TO RELAX**. Know the feeling of relaxed muscles. Memorize the feeling. You can recall that feeling whenever you find yourself growing tense when you are talking.

## Relaxation Exercise:

- Lie on your back on a bed or the floor

- Feet about twelve inches apart

- Hands, palms downward, about six inches from sides

- Concentrate on your left hand - tighten into a fist

- Do not tense the rest of the arm

- Relax it. Memorize the difference.

- Continue tightening and relaxing: hands arms, feet, legs, body.

- Feel the difference. Memorize the difference.

Remember almost everything you do you have **LEARNED** to do. So you can correct, enlarge, decrease, enhance your voice through training and concentration.

## Some Breathing Exercises:

First, do these breathing exercises lying on your back. This will help you keep those shoulders from rising as you take in a deep breath.

When you have felt the centring power, repeat, standing or sitting. It is important to repeat all exercises until your are comfortable that it has become a natural process for you and something you can do anywhere or anytime.

1. **Take in a breath quickly; hold for two counts and exhale as you say:**

   **a)** **AH**

   **b)** **SSSSSSS** (as if you were slowly and steadily letting air out of a balloon - as you push breath out you will feel the *'push'* from the mid-section.

   **c)** **ZZZZZZZZZ** (formed the same way as S) but voiced.

   **d)** Humming **M-M-M-M-M-M-M-M-M**

2. **Take in a breath:**

| IN | HOLD ( 1,2,3,4 ) | OUT |
|----|------------------|-----|
| quickly |  | quickly |
| quickly |  | slowly |
| slowly |  | slowly |
| slowly |  | quickly |

3.  **Count as far as you can on one breath.
    DO NOT SPEAK IN A MONOTONE.**

    Be careful to push from the centre. Watch the pace -
    speak at a normal speed. You should be able to count to
    at least forty-five on one breath. For variety you might
    try saying the months of the year or the days of the
    week, repeating until the breath is gone.

4.  **Repeat #3 whispering instead of using
    your voice.**

5.  **Place one hand on your side ribs and the
    other on the upper part of your stomach
    (just about where the rib cage starts to
    divide).**

    Breath in feeling the expansion width through the hands.

6.  **To develop the strength and flexibility of
    the diaphragm, take in a full breath and
    let it out as you pant "like a puppy".**

    Keep a hand on the midriff region feeling for the
    movement of the diaphragm.

7.  **Take in a deep breath and expel as you
    say HA - HA - HA - HA - (etc)**

    Be careful as you do this exercise. Use as little breath
    as possible.

    To control the outgoing breath you will have to
    concentrate on the abdominal muscles that skirt the
    waist and the diaphragm. Breathing exercises help
    you develop this ability.

8. **This exercise will help you 'top up' your breath supply while phrasing for sharing ideas not words.**

Read the following numbers aloud - pausing at each - 'dash'. Top up your breath at the dashes as needed.

**1 2 - 3 4 5 - 6 7 8 - 9 10**

**1 2 3 4 - 5 6 - 7 8 9 - 10**

**1 2 - 3 4 5 6 - 7 8 - 9 10**

**1 2 3 4 5 6 - 7 8 9 10**

**1 2 3 - 4 5 6 7 - 8 9 10 11 - 12 13 14 15 -**

**16 17 18 19 20**

9. **Read this passage aloud. Use a slash(/) to mark pauses. You can replenish / your breath / at any / of these stops. /**

*I believe in the dignity of labor, whether by head or hand. I believe that the world owes no man a living but that it owes every man an opportunity to make a living.*

John D. Rockefeller, July 8, 1941

Repeat until you are comfortable with the sound.

- Don't forget a good voice is just a breath away

- Practice until everything is a natural process

# POW ! - R
# Producing
# Vocal Exercises
# Using
# Projection

- **Take a sip of breath and exhale through closed teeth.**
  Try to keep the expulsion of breath even. Feel the diaphragm pulling in tighter and tighter.

- **Place hand in front of mouth - about eight inches away.**
  Purse lips as though you were going to whistle. Blow in a steady stream into centre of palm. Repeat with hand about twelve inches in front. Then again with hand at arms length.

**Are you muzzling
your potential**

# MATCH
# YOUR VOICE
# TO
# YOUR VISUAL
# IMAGE

Is your voice getting in the way of your message?

"Your voice paints a picture of you
in your listener's mind - make sure it's
the one you want there."

If you want to speak effectively you have to know where you are right now. *Speaking is a learned skill.* Much is learned by imitation. While you were developing your speaking habits you were particularly vulnerable to good and bad influences.

Have you ever had someone say "You sound just like your Mother," or "I thought it was your Dad when you answered the phone." You don't speak the way you speak because of your genes; it's because of the influences surrounding you. You imitate.

When it comes to your voice–you may be muzzling your potential!

## Remember:

- you can unlearn your bad habits
- you can learn and apply new positive speaking habits

## The most common problems with the way you sound:

You are:

- too fast
- too high
- a mumbler

- too slow
- too low
- a one-note wonder

If you are pleased with the way you sound, you are part of a very small group. Most people don't like the way they sound. Many people can't believe they sound that way! They protest, *"That isn't my voice!"*

As I said in the introduction–the voice you hear on your answering machine is the voice others hear.

Whenever you open your mouth and speak, those within earshot form a mental picture of you.

The sound of your voice will transmit an image faster than the speed of light!

**Bill Bernbach (1911-1982)** was considered a legend in his own time in the advertising field.

Here is what he said about speaking with **POW ! - R.**

> "The truth isn't the truth
> until they believe you;
> and they can't believe you
> if they don't know what you are saying;
> and they can't know what you are saying
> if they don't listen to you;
> and they won't listen to you
> if you're not interesting;
> and you won't be interesting
> unless you say things freshly,
> originally,
> and imaginatively."

On the following pages you'll find a few *"Images"* and the vocal problems that create them.

Check to see where you fit in - you may find a combinatination of problems.

Do the exercises suggested. Then you, too, can put your best voice forward.

| **PROBLEM** | **IMAGE** |
|---|---|

Talking too quickly

BUBBLE-HEAD BERTHA
or
MOTOR-MOUTH MAX

You'll sound nervous even if you are not. You give an impression of running off at the mouth without too much thought.

You have to speak at a pace that allows your listener to hear what you are saying, understand the words, and digest the information.

## How to Correct:

- Work on talking in **"ideas"**

- Pause between each spoken phrase.

- Read Shakespeare's sonnets or the Psalms. You cannot say these quickly.

- Take a piece of prose or some poetry. Hold it in your right hand; read the first word; transfer paper to your left hand ; read the next word. Do this a verse at a time.

- Next break into spoken phrases and read again.

- Repeat the phrases **BUT** break up differently. This will help you see you **CAN** stop between words and ideas.

| PROBLEM | IMAGE |
|---|---|

Using the upper tones in your voice register

LIGHT-WEIGHT LILY
or
LARRY

Although men have this problem too, it is particularly irritating in a woman's voice because women's voices tend to be higher.

Combined with too fast a pace you become a squeaker, a light weight, a person not to be taken seriously

## How to Correct:

- Use exercises for **"speaking too quickly"**

- Find your optimum pitch (see **PITCH KEY # 4**)

- Work on resonance (Mmm-Mmm-Mmm, etc.)

- Linger over your vowels. These are unstopped sounds. Give them the chance to resound as you say them. This gives tone to your voice.

- Example: Say "see the sea" stretching the long "EE" sound.

- Say **"How are you"** stretching the **'ow' 'a' 'ou'**

- You won't talk this way in normal conversation. You must extend your sounds so you will feel comfortable giving them the duration they need to colour your speech.

| **PROBLEM** | **IMAGE** |
|---|---|

Using lower tones all the time

POMPOUS PETER
or
PONDEROUS PETULA

Again this can be a problem for both men and women. It is particularly annoying in a man's voice. They are normally lower. However, people who stay "low down" may have been told low and slow voices gives an air of command; of thoughtful comment.

It can also give you the label of pseudo-intellectual! It can make you appear unapproachable.

When it is combined with poor articulation you sound like a Rumbler or Mumbler par excellence!

## How to Correct:

- Find your optimum pitch. (see **PITCH KEY #4**)
  Move your initiating tone up the scale.

- Work on varying your pace.

- 'Lift' your voice by smiling whenever you can.
  The resonating shape in your mouth will change.

- Check your vocabulary. Slow speakers often equate four syllable words with intellect!

- Work on tongue twisters for effective, clear articulation.

44

| PROBLEM | IMAGE |
|---|---|

The "grey" voice

JOHNNY-ONE -NOTE
or
JANEY-ONE-NOTE

Such a voice can give out an image of a robot; a boring or bored person; someone who is dull-witted, depressed, tired, or uninterested.

The average speaker has a vocal range of at least two octaves. That's at least two dozen pitches.

Grey speakers only use one or perhaps two. Most people only use two or three.

## How to Correct:

- You need to colour your voice.
  Say **"OH"** as you picture someone giving you a beautiful gift, saying you're fired, picking up a smiling infant.

- Add your own scenarios to allow you to vocalize surprise, impatience, anger or whatever.

- Concentrate on the Four P's.

  1. **PITCH** - new idea, new pitch - higher or lower

  2. **PACE** - faster or slower

  3. **PAUSE** - for thought breaks and breath

  4. **PROJECTION** - think out and speak with energy!

| **PROBLEM** | **IMAGE** |

The "Sock-it-to-me"
Voice

MACK
or
MINNIE THE MUMBLER

Most mumblers forget
articulation takes place at the
front of the mouth most of
the time.

The sounds you make
are created by utilizing the
various organs of articulation.
They are your lips, teeth, jaw,
gum ridge, hard and soft
palates, and most important -
your tongue.

The sound comes out through your mouth (exceptions "m,n,
and ng" sounds). If you keep your mouth stationary, with the
lips and jaws not moving, the sound is muffled.

Mumblers often wonder why no one understands what
they are saying. They might succeed as ventriloquists...but
not as effective speakers.

## How to Correct:

- Exercise all your organs of articulation.
  They must be flexible and free.

- Say **OO-EE-OO-EE** several times.
  Feel the movement in the lips.

- Say **AH-AYE-AH-AYE** several times to help loosen the
  jaw.

- Work on pitch. Most mumblers are also
  pseudo-monotones.

Breathiness

HEART ATTACK HARRY
or
SEX-POT SUE

This quality often goes along with the quiet tone in women speakers.

It might work on an after midnight radio show. It has no place in business.

If you're a man you can sound like a wheezer or gasper.

If you ever use a microphone when you speak you'll have people more interested in knowing if you'll last through the talk.

What you say will be whisked away in great puffs of uncontrolled breath.

## How to Correct:

- Work on breath support and control.

- Work on re-enforcing tone.

- Work on projection.

- Make sure your pace suits your subject.
  Women in particular have a tendency to combine breathiness with a too fast overall pace.

| **PROBLEM** | **IMAGE** |
|---|---|
| Too loud | SALLY THE SHOUTER<br>or<br>BOSSY BOB |

Such a voice suggests to listeners a person who is bossy, or narrow-minded.

Someone who doesn't want to hear anyone else's ideas.

It suggests someone who has a hand on the horn all time.

A "My-way-or-no-way" person. A talker who won't listen.

## How to Correct:

- You might start by having your hearing checked. Some people talk loudly because they have difficulty hearing.

- Work on projection. Loudness is often the result of pushing from the throat instead of from the diaphragm.

- Develop a sensitivity to your surroundings and listener. Remember a nudge will get you the attention you want more quickly than a push.

- Work on modulation. Loudness is often caused by **pushing** words for emphasis instead of **'lifting'** the words out. Working with the **Four P's** will help you.

- Listen when people say "Don't talk so loudly". You want to Pow!-R-Talk **BUT** in control!

Tight jaw delivery

TOUGH TALKING TED
or
SULKY SARAH

Do not lock your jaw or tighten your lips, tongue throat .

You will not only look as if you are continually unhappy, you will sound that way.

This habit is usually one of long standing. Often such speakers grind their teeth at night.

## How to Correct:

- This problem is caused by muscle tension in the jaw, neck and upper torso. If your back molars are touching you have this tension.

- You need to work on relaxation. There must be some space at the back of your mouth - between the upper and lower jaws. The lower jaw "hangs loose".

- Yawn. Feel the flexibility of your jaw. Massage the points at the sides of your face where the upper and lower jaws meet.

- Say AH-EE-AH-EE-AH-EE, stretching the muscles of your face.

- Tight-jawed people often have 'frozen' faces, too. Remember this order; feel it, think it, see it, then say it.

49

Pushing voice into nasal passages

WILLY
or
WINNIE THE WHINER

Except for the sounds "m", "n", and "ng", all sound is projected through the mouth.

A tight jaw or closed mouth leaves your voice with no alternative. It will come out your nose!

Try saying "I'm so happy" while pushing the sound through the nose. The message sounds so insincere it's laughable.

Sportscasters often end up using a nasal tone. They may be able to get away with it. Most people just sound whiny, unhappy, unsure of themselves.

## How to Correct:

- Hum MMMMMM-AH sustaining the AH. While you are doing this, place your forefingers on either side of your nose. You will feel a vibration with the MMMMMM. If it is there when you say AH - you have some nasality.

- Keep your the soft palate high to stop the sound from going into the nasal passages.

- Yawn. While you are yawning say AH.
  Take a breath and repeat saying OH

- Say K-K-K-K-K and G-G-G-G-G.
  Say gurgle, gurgle, gurgle.

- Try to imitate the **"glugging"** sound liquid makes when you turn a bottle upside down and the liquid comes out in spurts.

| PROBLEM | IMAGE |
|---------|-------|

Too soft spoken

INDECISIVE IVAN
or
INSECURE IDA

If people often ask you to repeat your comment, if you have the feeling "no one ever listens to me!", it may be because you make it too difficult.

You may be shy. You may have been brought up to equate refinement with a quiet tone. You may have been encouraged to "speak softly!".

You may even try to use the soft tone for effect. Speak quietly and people **HAVE** to listen? Unfortunately people are lazy listeners. Give them half a chance and they will turn you off.

## How to Correct:

- Use your tape recorder. Place the microphone about eighteen inches away. Project your voice into the mic, pushing the voice from the diaphragm, not the throat.

- Count to five in your normal tone. Count to five in a whisper. (No voicing allowed. Whisper must be audible at least ten feet away.) Count to five again - normal voice. Note the stronger projection. Repeat X3.

- Count to ten. Pull each number out of your mouth as if it was stuck to a wad of bubble gum. Alternate your hands and keep your eye on the 'wad' as you say each number.

- Play a piece of music as you record your voice. Project into the mic without shouting or straining.

- **You can change your vocal image. You have already been introduced to the first step. POW ! - R Breathing. You need four more "P's" to Power Speak. That's Key Number Four.**

I am sure you will spot many different speaking voices in your life in the past couple of pages. Some have probably annoyed you and perhaps you didn't quite understand why.

Also, you may not quite find your voice group and may be a combination of one or two different voice types.

If this is the case, in the following space draw your *"type"* and some points as to what you want to correct. See if you can come up with some ideas to correct these points.

## Cooper Coomunicating Tool

- **You can't say things freshly, orginally, and imaginatively if you do not speak with a voice that is full, flexible, friendly and forceful.**

**KEY NO. 4**

Pitch - Pace - Pause - Projection

# YOUR
# FOUR P's
# FOR PEAK
# PERFORMANCE

Control these **FOUR P's** and your voice will take a great leap forward.

"The English Language is a stress language! You can change the meaning of what you say by the way you say it."

- **PITCH**

- **PACE**

- **PAUSE**

- **PROJECTION**

As you learn to use these tools you will start developing the sound you want in your voice. Thus you will gain a voice people will want to listen to.

**THE FOUR P's** combined with **POWER**, give you the basic tools you need to power talk. When you use these tools you clarify your meaning, you also change your phrasing.

Spoken phrases are different from grammatical written phrases. Too many people depend on **VOLUME** alone to make particular words stand out. This can make your voice an ear-bashing hammer.

Pretty soon your listeners are only conscious of the hammering! They tune you out to stop the pain. **THE MESSAGE IS LOST!!**

### Cooper Communicating Tool

- **Too many speakers think of the words they are saying instead of the thoughts they want to share.**

Because English is a stress language you can change the meaning of what you are saying by how you say it.

**Example:**

| | | |
|---|---|---|
| **Barbara** | loves | Bob. |
| Barbara | **loves** | Bob. |
| Barbara | loves | **Bob**. |

**To get your point across, every time you have a new idea, you MUST:**

| | | |
|---|---|---|
| ● change your | **PITCH** | Move it higher or lower |
| ● change your | **PACE** | Make it faster or slower |
| ● be sure to | **PAUSE** | A momentary hesitation before and/or after the word(s) you are highlighting. |
| ● and use | **PROJECTION** | Use your power base to push your voice forward and out with tone and clarity. |

● **A new idea is another way of saying a new spoken phrase. Spoken phrases are different from grammar or written phrases.**

Before going into detail on **PITCH, PACE, PAUSE** and **PROJECTION** you need to think about phrasing effectively.

When you tie proper phrasing and inflection to orchestrating your voice you have the basic tools.

Apply these to your four P's and your speaking power will quickly move into high gear.

## Definitions:

a.  A *spoken phrase* is *any* word or a group of words uttered on one breath impulse to convey a single idea or train of thought.

b.  A *written phrase* is a group of words related in some way and not containing a subject and verb.

## Some examples of SPOKEN PHRASES:

- The old **MAN**/ walked across the **STREET**/ to get his **DOG.**

- The **OLD** man/ **WALKED**/ across the street to get his dog.

- **THE**/ old **MAN**/ walked **ACROSS**/ the street to **GET**/ **HIS** dog.

Your inner thoughts dictate the spoken phrasing. Change your focus and you change your phrasing.

You direct your listener to the **SPECIFIC** way you want that person to interpret the words!

To phrase properly you must focus on your message. Know what you want your listener(s) to **DO** after you've spoken. **THEN** - Use these four power tools to help you express your ideas effectively!

56

# HOW DO YOU
# DO THIS?

Think of your words the way you picture musical notes on sheet music.

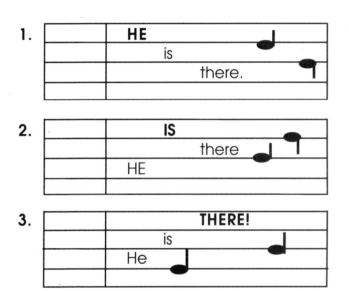

### Note:

You do not have to use a higher pitch. You will be equally effective moving the pitch down.

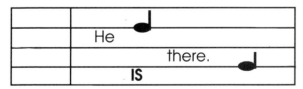

● **The key is FLEXIBILITY**

Within each phrase you *"work the sounds"*. Take a sentence and break it into ideas or trains of thought.

## Example:

- Too many people / think of the words / instead of / the thoughts / they want to share.

Which word is most important in each train?

## Example:

- **TOO MANY** people/ think of the **WORDS/INSTEAD** of/ the **THOUGHTS**/ they want to **SHARE.**

In that one sentence you have **FIVE** different ideas or spoken phrases. By switching pitches and 'working the words' you make it easy for people to listen.

Help them to understand even more easily. *"Curve"* your words using inflection.

**INFLECTION** is a sliding of your voice through several pitches within a word in one continuing sound. It is an easy voice technique to acquire and use.

## Two things to remember about inflection:

1. There are three basic ways to inflect your voice.

- **Rising**
  Voice slides upwards.

  Oh ↗

- **Falling**
  Voice slides downward.

  Oh ↘

- **Circumflex**
  Voice moves up and down within the sound.

  Oh ∧∨↗

**2.** ● **A rising inflection**
Suggests an incomplete thought. It is weak.

● **A falling inflection**
Suggests a complete thought.
It suggests certainty. You are in control.

**Cooper Communicating Tool**

● **Do not "rise to the occasion"!**

● **Always use a falling inflection at the end of spoken phrases. It gives your comments strength.**

● **Do this even when asking a question!**

Say *"I will"* with a rising then a falling inflection. and hear the difference. Here is a simple way to get started.

### Exercise:

1. Look around you. Identify aloud some of the items you see. For example **"shoes"**, **"window"**, **"wall"**, **"pen"**. **"computer"**. (You can see I'm in my office as I write this!)

While you say these words - hold your hand up as if you were going to conduct an orchestra.
    As you say each word, move your hand up and down in a half-circle. It will help you *'orchestrate'* your words.

**2.** Say in turn each of these words
**OH...NO...WHY...YES...STOP**
while you picture something that makes you
feel the following emotion :
**Fear. Anger. Happiness. Surprise.**

## Example:

- Imagine you are opening a door.

- As you open it say "OH!" as you would if
  someone was there with a huge present for
  you.

- Repeat as you picture someone at the door
  with whom you are very angry.

**3.** Another way to "**work at inflection**": Read the
following single words to reflect the thoughts that
are in brackets. Note how your inflection changes.

**Yes** (that is what happened)
**Yes** (Well - I think that is what happened)

**No** (I won't do it - now or ever!)
**No** (Is that really true!)

**Stop** (don't move one inch from where you are!)
**Stop** (After all the work I've put in so far?)

You are speaking to get a message to the person or people
listening. Using these tools and others you'll obtain as you
work with this book will help you do just that.

Remember **LISTENERS ARE LAZY.** They may get
up to forty or fifty percent of your message if they are
**REALLY** listening. Most people will catch about twenty to
twenty-five percent of what you say. *By using these power
tools you will be sure they get the essence for action.*

Most of our words are *'joiner'* words. Take this story for example: Read it emphasizing the bolded words.

> ● Once upon a time there was lovely young **princess** and a handsome **prince**. The princess had a little brown **dog**. The dog had **three spots** on his **back**.

Only six of the twenty-eight words are really important; **"princess/prince/dog/three spots/back".** They carry the essence of the message. The rest are *'joiners',* they are necessary but are not important to this interpretation of the message.

When you change the interpretation - the key words change. Read it again emphasizing the new bolded words.

> ● Once upon a time there **was** a lovely **young** princess and a **handsome** prince. The princess had a **little** brown **dog**. The dog had **three** spots on **his** back.

By using ***Pitch, Pace and Pause*** effectively you select the way you want your message to be remembered.

With your voice you must do what you would do with punctuation marks if you were writing.

By modulating your voice, you insert the periods, commas, quotation marks, exclamation marks and question marks. Your voice **'bolds'** the words to make them stand out. Your voice <u>underlines</u> to make a point stand out.

● **Your voice will make some words <u>S T A N D O U T</u> simply by the way you say them!!!! By using projection you make sure the message is heard easily.**

When you use the **FOUR P's** properly you are more effective **AND** your energy is directed towards the positive results you want - *after you finish talking.*

# DETAILS ON THE FOUR P's

## PITCH - What is it?

Pitch is the position of your voice on your vocal scale.

Most people have a pitch range of at least two octaves. **MOST PEOPLE USE ONLY TWO OR THREE NOTES IN THEIR RANGE!** This is one reason it is difficult to listen to most voices. The speaker stays on the same pitch no matter how many new thoughts are being presented.

Picture a machine tracking someone's heartbeat. The screen looks like this:

As long as that line moves up and down you know that person is alive. When the machine starts to put out this signal:

You know the heart has stopped. Energy is **ZERO.**

● **If you let your voice stretch out in a never ending straight line, you take ITS life away. You have taken the heart out of what you**

Even if your listeners manage to keep listening you run another risk. They will interpret your message **THEIR WAY.**

Work to change your pitch each time you introduce new ideas. Your listeners will relax and absorb your message.

## Exercises to Develop Pitch Awareness:

● Count from **TEN** to **ONE** moving down a pitch with each number **THEN** go back up the scale.

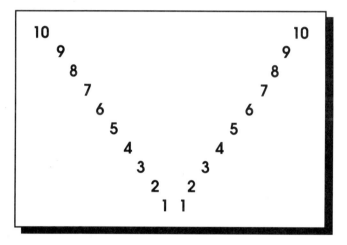

Repeat. You will find it very easy to move up and down this modified vocal scale. *It represents only about a third of the pitch range you have!*

Despite this capability, I repeat, most people use two or three pitches when speaking!

No wonder people have developed poor listening habits. Who wants to listen to dull talk? Would you listen to a singer who used only two or three notes all the time? Or a musician?

● **Your voice is an instrument. Learn to play it well and you will speak symphonies!**

## Pitch Exercise:

# ● Orchestrating Your Message

Your speaking voice and your singing voice are the same. The only difference is you 'hold' the sung note longer.

In these sentences, march up and down the scale as shown here.

- ● The word (or words) you wish to dominate will be at the top or bottom of your chart.
- ● Read them once then change the orchestration and do again.

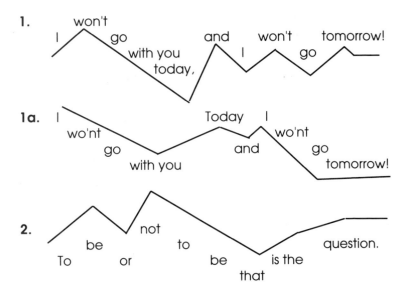

## ● What is your PITCH RANGE?

Here's a simple way to discover it .You need a piano or similar instrument to sound the initial note.

- ● Sound **MIDDLE C** on the piano. Using a full chest of breath, sing that note. (**Remember:** sung notes and spoken notes are the same; you simply hold sung notes longer).

- ● Move down the notes singing each note and half-note on a new breath.

- ● When you've gone as low as you can with a full breath, mark that note and go back to **MIDDLE C**.

- ● Repeat - going up the scale to the highest note you can reach. Mark it. You now know your vocal range.

## ● You now need to determine your OPTIMUM PITCH and HABITUAL PITCH

Everyone has an **HABITUAL PITCH**. This is the pitch you generally use when you start to speak. The **OPTIMUM PITCH** is the one you should be using. Ideally they should be one and the same. *If they are not, you cannot make the best use of your vocal range*

Here is how to discover your Optimum Pitch. Look at the lowest note on your vocal range.

Count up **ONE-THIRD** of the way towards the top note you reached. *That is your Optimum Pitch.*

- ● If you are initiating sound two tones or half-tones above or below this optimum pitch you must try to adjust. If you do not, you are limiting the use of the POW ! - R Speech you possess.

## PACE - What is it?

Pace is the time you take to say words and/or phrases. Some people refer to it as the *'Tempo of your Talk'.* Others may call it the *'Rate'.*

To speak effectively you must look at *two areas* for proper pacing.

> 1.  The **over-all pace** at which you speak.
>
> 2.  The **time it takes** you to say a word.

- ## The Most Important Aspect of PROPER PACING is VARIETY

With each new idea there is a change of **PITCH** and **PACE.**

- ## The Over-All PACE

Just remember **H.U.D.** Speak so your listener can:

> a)  **Hear** what you are saying.
>
> b)  **Understand** both words and meaning.
>
> c)  **Digest** the information for effective action.

### Cooper Communicating Tool

- **Notice how you S T R E T C H the vowels in the words you choose to emphasize; how you take longer to say the word you want to 'LIFT OUT'.**

66

## ● Pace FLEXIBILITY Within Words

Sounds in the English language vary. Simply put, some are short - some are long. It takes longer to say *"prolong"* than it does to say *"instant"*. To fully utilize **PACE** use words that create the images you want.

For example take the word **WATER.** You can create many images about water through the words you use to describe it. It can *gush, meander, drip, gurgle.* It can be *rough, calm, choppy, placid.*

Many words in the English language paint special pictures by their sounds; by the pace or duration used.

By changing the *'duration'* you lift out or emphasize certain words.

Change the word you emphasize and you change the intent of what you say! The following exercise demonstrates this tool. Try it.

### Exercise:

Using your tape recorder, say each of the sentences several times. Each time *"lift"* out a different word, give examples. Listen to the results. Have you conveyed different ideas and meanings simply through the use of the **4 P's?**

| | |
|---|---|
| 1. | Is she the person you said you saw. |
| 2. | Mary is quite fond of Ronald. |
| 3. | Vincent, would you like the present? |
| 4. | A bird in the hand is worth two in the bush. |
| 5. | What do you think she will do to them. |
| 6. | Speak now or forever hold your peace. |

To *"program"* your mind to automatically do this for you, you first have to practice **"LIFTING"**.

Here's a **DAILY** exercise to help you develop this technique. Take a story or editorial from a newspaper, or a magazine. Look at the first sentence. *Read it aloud several times, changing the emphasis each time.*

Another simple exercise. Do it when you are stopped at a stop light while driving!

Say:

> **The** light will turn green.
>
> The **light** will turn green.
>
> The light **will** turn green.
>
> The light will **turn** green.
>
> The light will turn **green.**

By the time you say this the light will turn green.

## Cooper Communicating Tool

● **Remember - you carry your voice with you. You can practice on this 'INSTRUMENT' whenever you have a few free minutes. You'll soon see powerful results from the minutes you utilize throughout the day to keep it tuned.**

## PAUSE - A Powerful Tool

● **Why are so many speakers afraid to pause?**

They feel they are *d-r-a-g-g-i-n-g o-u-t* what they want to say. Seconds of silence often seem endless. Also, most people think they are not experienced speakers. So when they *'raise their voices'* in public or in business they want to say what they have to say quickly and get it over.

Pace and pause really work together. Sometimes you use the stretching technique for emphasis and pacing. Most often you use this in combination with pause.

When you stretch a word for emphasis you should balance this with a longer pause.

## NOTE:

Often people who speak too quickly try to correct this by using longer pauses. The result is a choppy, disjointed delivery. Pauses help you in various ways to communicate more effectively.

If you want your listener to really *'get the message'* you must allow opportunities to digest it. Your pauses do this.

Think of feeding a baby its food. You give the child a spoonful - wait for it to be swallowed - then offer another.

What happens when you are in a hurry! You spoon the food in too quickly. If you are lucky it just runs out the sides of the mouth!

One thing is certain. The food isn't swallowed; the nourishment is gone.

This is what happens when you don't pause to let the listeners digest your message. Your audience may *hear* every word but you want them to absorb your message. Pausing lets the message sink in.

**PAUSING** and **PHRASING** must work together. Keep the phrases short (six words or less remember) and pause between the ideas.

A pause not only keeps ideas separated and hi-lights ideas - it gives you opportunities to top up your breath supply.

Use pauses effectively and you will always be speaking from a strong *POW ! - R Base.*

# PROJECTION

- **"Speak up. I can't hear you!"**

A common complaint. Unfortunately most speakers respond by speaking louder. By using loudness or volume to try to get the message out, too often is a message directed *'at'* you instead of one directed 'to' you.

To project your voice effectively you must force more air through your vocal cords. The **KEY is THROUGH** the vocal cords. The air must be driven from the diaphragm.

And open your mouth when you speak. You need somewhere for that sound to go!

Projection allows you to reach your listener without raising your voice. Do not push the sound from the throat. Use Pow!-R-Centring!. Rest your hand lightly on your centre. Pretend you are "ho-ho-hoing" like Santa Claus. Feel the diaphragm and abdominal muscles push the breath and sound out. You are projecting.

Proper projection results from a proper mental attitude also. Once you know you can power your breath you know you have the strength to send the sound where you want it.

I remember when my boys were young I was the *"Child Caller"* of the neighbourhood. Without straining I would *'project'* my voice up or down the block and call not only my children home, but anyone else's. They couldn't get their voices to carry that far for all their shouting!

**PROJECTION** and **INTENSITY** are closely tied. The latter is that vibrant quality conveying emotion and commitment to what you say. It does not depend upon loudness or upon raised pitch; just the reverse. When you speak in a whisper with feeling and conviction your message may be far more intense.

Have you ever tried speaking quietly, but with purpose,

when reprimanding someone? Then you know what I mean. The quiet, projected tone is much more effective. Again it depends on the feeling behind the words; the message you want to convey.

If you want to reach the back row of your audience - consciously direct your words out there. Your *power centring* and *power techniques* will carry the words. Your intensity and projection will carry the message. Here are some projection exercises to help you.

1. **Imagine someone is walking away from you.**

   - Call out stop - stop - stop several times as they move away.

   - Do not shout. Project to the imaginary retreating back.

2. **Pretend you are giving numbers to a line of people:**

   - Without raising your voice give them numbers up to twenty.

3. **Picture a group of youngsters in front of you. In a normal tone say:**

   - "If you all sit still I will read you a story".

   - Another row of children sits down. Project the message to them.

   - Continue this as rows of children come and sit until they are in the next room.

   - Remember to keep the volume and pitch down.

   - Concentrate on projecting from your power centre.

4. **Inhale slowly and fill the lungs before saying each of the following:**

- "Ouch!"
- "Now"
- "Taxi!"
- "I can't hear you"

5. **<u>To help you train your brain</u>.
The diaphragm will respond automatically if you give it a chance. Your projection will be appropriate for the space and situation.**

- "Hold that elevator!"
- "Would you please be quiet.  They can hear you in the board room"
- "Would those standing at the back of the room come to these front chairs,  please."
- "Let's slip out the side door so we won't disturb the others."

6. **<u>To help place the tone forward in the mouth</u>.
Use forward consonant sounds to help you feel the forward placement.**

V = Voice
B = Breath

- FAH  FAY  FEE  FI  FOH  FOO      **V**
  VAH  VAY  VEE  VI  VOH  VOO     **B**

- SAH  SAY  SEE  SI  SOH  SOO      **V**
  ZAH  ZAY  ZEE  ZI  ZOH  ZOO    **B**

- LAH  LAY  LEE  LI  LOH  LOO      **V**

- THAH  THAY  THEE  THI  THOH  THOO   **VB**

Here are some final reminders and ideas to help you shape up your voice and *Power Talk.*

## 1. KNOW YOUR VOICE

Tape it and shape it. You have to hear how you sound to others. Tape a paragraph from a talk you're preparing. Take a paragraph from a printed article or newspaper. Read it and tape it. Listen and observe. Correct problems and repeat until you sound enthused and your message is clearly carrying your meaning.

## 2. GO ON A POWER TRIP

Centre your breathing. Your *POW ! - R Talking* starts with the diaphragm. Say, "Watch out!" as if you were stopping someone from falling into a deep hole. Pretend they are a little distance away. Push that voice out from your *'voice centre'* just about your navel. Feel that power; feel where it is located; memorize the feeling.

## 3. GET IN SHAPE

Get your vowels and consonants working for you. Use your long vowel sounds. Stretch them. They give the colour and meaning to your words. Change them from words to pictures.

Try this. Think about your feet. What can you do with them? You can 'stroll'; 'jog'; 'wander; 'walk briskly', 'hesitantly', 'slowly'. Tape the words. Listen. Hear how the sound ties in with the meaning. That is *'shaping your sounds for speaking success'.*

## 4. SIGN THE PLEDGE

Swear never to resort to "whine" again. You develop this sound when you use too high a pitch. Women are more prone to whining. Men also slip into this weak sound. Work with your middle and lower tones. They carry much more conviction.

## 5. DON'T PLAY TAG

Here's are examples of 'tagging'. Don't weaken your words!

- "It's a good plan, *don't you think?*"

- "It's hard to give speeches, *isn't it?*"

**KEY NO. 5**

**Focusing for
first-rate impact**

# THE
# P.R.E.P. / T.R.I.M.
# PROCESS

Prepare - then trim off the extras.

"Fail to plan and you
Plan to fail."

The *first four keys to Speaking with Confidence look at you*. The way you sound. The *next four concentrate on the reason you speak. Your audience and your message.*

You speak to share ideas. You want your listeners to accept those ideas. To buy. To try. To act on your information. To choose you and your plans.

That is why you must make your speaking techniques part of you. How you speak must become automatic. It will, if you spend time each day working with the first four keys.

With your voice under control, you can concentrate on your message. Your message must be orchestrated as carefully as your voice.

To know how to say what you say to gain your objectives you have to start with the bottom line.

- **What do I want my listeners(s) to know or do when I stop talking**

Using the **P.R.E.P / T.R.I.M** approach you will not miss a note when *'arranging'* your message for the results you want.

Whether you are talking to one person or one hundred and one people.

- **To succeed you must prepare - P.R.E.P.
You must also be concise - T.R.I.M.**

Here's the score!

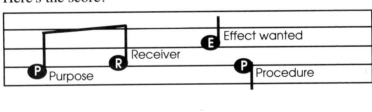

# **P** urpose / **T** arget

- ● Why are you talking?
- ● What do you want to happen as a result of what you say?

*Decide this first.* Then you'll be able to make your *"road map".* You will have a tangible target.

# **R** eceiver / **R** eader

Successful speakers identify with their audiences. To do this they analyze them. This is a key element in *Pow!-R Speaking - Key 6.* You'll find full directions for analysing your audience there.

Just remember:

- ● The more you know about your audience the easier it is to focus effectively.

- ● Without focus you have no direction - no goal. Neither has your listener. The message will fall on unreceptive ears!

# **E** ffect / **I** mpact

Do you want your audience to buy? Try? March? Laugh? Hire you? Fire someone else? Give you the job? Accept your idea? Have faith in your decision?

*Know what you want before you start preparing your presentation!*

## Reminder:

For this you need **ACTION GOALS -**

- **When I am finished I want my listener(s)
to do this, this, and this**

You **ALWAYS** know what you want to say. If you have nothing to say you don't speak! *It isn't enough to know what you are talking about!!!!* You have to know what you want your listener(s) to do with the information you are sharing.

- **The key to speaking success is successfully combining effective speaking skills with the organizing of your ideas to get the action you want.**

## Example of organizing for the action you want:

You are presenting a report.

- **Focus 1**
  You want the 'listeners' to give you another $50,000 dollars and another six months for further research

- **Focus 2**
  You want them to take the findings and put them into action.

You will present the same information. However, it will be presented *differently in each case to get the action you want.*

- **Focus 1**

  would stress the groundwork; the new discoveries which need exploring for effective exploiting; an optimistic focus on a worthwhile endeavor deserving the extra time and money to reap the fullest rewards for the audience.

- **Focus 2**

  would stress the above but the focus would be on "**time to move from theory to practical application**".

- **Knowing the effect you want determines the way you prepare**

# **P** rocedure / **M** ethod

Once you have decided why you are speaking, to whom your remarks are directed, and why you want your remarks listened to, your job is simple. You will know how to organize it. You can concentrate on such things as:

## Logical order of your presentation

- Visual aids needed? What kind? Handouts? Pre-talk distribution of background?

- One person/two people/group presentation?

Now it is time to focus in on **_Presenting - and Connecting_** when you present.

First you need to know what a **_"Presentation"_** is!

## There are three general types of presentation situations

1. **One-to-one**
   **(in person or on a telephone)**

2. **Informal meetings**
   **( in a  meeting room, a coffee shop,**
   **or even around your kitchen table)**

3. **Lectern or platform presentations**

The situations are different. The focus is not. Unless you are in the habit of talking to yourself, remember - every time you speak to another person or a group of people you are **_"presenting"_** an idea.

You are **_"communicating"_** your thoughts. You do this for one reason only. You want those listening to buy in to your ideas. To do this you must make sure you are: **CONNECTING WHEN YOU SPEAK.**

When you speak you already know what you want to talk about. You're qualified to talk about it.

If you think you are not, you'd do well to remember the adage

"Better to stay silent and be thought a fool than to speak and prove the point".

Your skills as a communicator go far beyond what you say. The key to success lies in the way you present your ideas.

## Ask yourself these questions when you are preparing to give a presentation

1. Who am I speaking to?

2. Why?

3. What should I talk about?

4. How do I organize it to achieve my purpose?

5. How do I get myself ready?

6. What do I do to control the 'space' I'll be using?

7. What do I do to harness my 'nerves'?

8. How do I keep interest up while presenting?

9. How can I make "facts and figures" interesting to the listener(s)?

10. How do I get the response I want from the listener(s)?

Answer these questions **THEN** start orchestrating your message. When you do this you are *"orchestrating for success"*. You have addressed all necessary areas to make your presentation do what you want it to do.

Some of these questions have already been answered for you in your eight keys.

The next couple of pages will be partly review and partly new.

# Common Connection Problems and How to Correct them

1. No initial rapport with listener(s)

2. Energy level low

3. Poor, unclear speech

4. body stiff; face in neutral

5. Inability to use silence for impact

6. No eye contact - thinking "I" instead of "U"

7. Audience not involved emotionally

8. Language not suited to audience

9. Direction of presentation muddy

10. Speaker transmits personal fear of speaking before a group (or one-to-one)

Below are listed the details of common connection problems and how to correct them.

## 1. No initial rapport with listener(s)

You must *'connect'* right away. The first twenty words are more important than the next 20,000! Make sure your opening words grab and direct your listener.

**KNOW WHAT YOU ARE GOING TO START WITH.** Don't let it be *"Thank you for inviting me!"* If you feel you want to say this, or give greetings to special guests - alright. BUT - then break those words away from your *"presentation"*. Change your position. Move left or right.

Take out your script or notes. Put them on the lectern. Have an obvious pause - **THEN GIVE THOSE IMPORTANT FIRST WORDS...CONNECTING WITH SOMEONE (or more) IN YOUR AUDIENCE AS YOU SAY THEM.**

## 2. Energy Level low

The biggest problem of most speakers! How can you energize others when you don't speak with vigour! This does not mean you must be **LOUD!** It means working with the Four P's (Key 4) to project your voice and your ideas.

You must learn to *'call up'* that energy with a mental snap of your fingers. You do this by doing energy raising exercises every day for three weeks. (Pushups; skipping 20 times; punching an imaginary punching bag or person) You are then patterning or programming your brain to respond to your call. You cannot be the effective speaker you want to be without this energy.

It is also essential, of course, that you are really enthused about what you are saying. You must believe in your ideas passionately if you want others to go along with you!

## 3. Poor, unclear Speech

If people have to strain to understand you they will stop listening. It's as simple as that! There is no reason for any person to mumble and mutter. To speak with such a heavy accent your listener cannot understand.

Every sound in the English language is pronounced by using your breath and articulators a certain way. You can only say the sound *'p'* as in pop by putting your lips together; holding back the sound until you release it.

As you do there is a slight explosion or breath - the *'p'* sound. If you do the same thing and use your vocal cords you form the letter *'b'* as in bob. Put your articulators to work and your speech will be clear.

This does not mean you will not have a distinct way of speaking. We all have some sounds we say in special ways. It depends on the various influences which have affected our pronunciations.

As long as people understand you when you say ***"either"* as *'ee-ther'* or *'eye-ther'*** the way you say it doesn't matter. If your listeners have to interpret - they will very quickly stop listening. It is too much hard work!

## 4. Body stiff/wooden

If you tense - people think you are tense. Your listener will interpret that as a sign of nervousness. If you are uneasy - your audience will be too.

Practice speaking in front of a mirror. Remember the five phases of speech practice - ***Relaxating; POW ! - R-Breathing; Resonating; Articulating; Practicing.*** Practice relaxation exercises every day. Three minutes three times a day is not much to pay for the rewards you'll reap as a speaker who is confident and whose voice shows it.

## 5. Inability to use silence for impact

This is one of the all important *"Four P's"*. The pause. Give people a chance to absorb what you are saying. If you don't - they won't!

## 6. No eye contact/poor facial expression

Another of the important keys to effective PowerSpeaking. Remember the rules you've learned:

### Cooper Communicating Tool

**"Before you speak**

- **FEEL IT in your heart**
- **THINK IT in your head"**
- **SEE IT in your inner mind's eye**
- **and only then SAY IT!**

## 7. Audience not involved emotionally

Do not depend on logic alone to convince. Most people make decisions emotionally and justify them logically.

Do not leave out the logic but remember to touch as many senses as you can.

- "Picture this" "Look at it like this..."

- " I hear what you're saying."

- "You'll find you will feel right... "

## 8. Language not suited to audience

Talk to get your point across. You don't need to use four syllable words just to make an impression.

Do not use *'jargon'* unless your listeners fully under stand it. Churchill said *"Never use a pound word when a penny one will do."* Translate this into your own currency, but, remember the advice!

When you are presenting a talk or report remember you are talking. If you are using notes or a script make sure it is written in *'talk-writing'.* Short, simple sentences.

## 9. Direction of presentation muddy

Once you have decided your reason for speaking, your presentation will have focus only if you keep going back to **"WHAT DO I WANT THEM TO DO WHEN I STOP TALKING".**

- **Use the logical order you need to get that action.**
- **Leave out any information not related to your purpose.**

## 10. Speaker transmits personal fear of speaking before a group (or one-to-one)

Review Step 2. Direct that nervous energy into your message. Remember concentrate on your audience. What you want them to do with the information you are sharing, Your brain can then work with you and for you.

# Why do Presentations Fail?

Before you blame an unreceptive audience when they do not buy into your ideas - look at youself and your presentation! Here are some reasons presentations do not reach the goals of the presenters. **AVOID THEM.**

- Starting from "This is what I want to say!" Instead of "This is what I NEED to say to get my listener to "buy in."

- Speaking with poor vocal and physical skills including: Monotone; Pace that's too fast or too slow; Pitch too high or too low; No energy, enthusiasm or projection; no facial expression; No eye contact.

- Assuming you know your audience without checking for various sub-groups.

- Trying to cover too much material! Going into too much unnecessary detail.

- Not including listening directions for your listener(s) in your opening remarks.

- Straying from your focus.

- Assuming the audience is as interested as you are in the subject.

- Using jargon not familiar to your audience.

- Using unfamiliar words when you can just as easily use simpler ones.

- Ignoring obvious reactions from your audience.

- Using overly detailed visuals: too many visuals.

- Giving your audience material to read while you are trying to talk.

- Answering questions in a long, drawn-out way.

- Assuming everything you want to say is important to your audience or necessary to share with them to achieve your goals.

# What Makes a Presentation Powerful?

- It is organized, complete, and concise.
- It always ties the presentation to benefits for the listener.
- It shows the presenter has analyzed the audience.
- It is organized for the action wanted.

> 1. logical order
> 2. follows a road map or format
> 3. focused on station WII-FM (What's In It For Me)
> 4. replaces "I" with "YOU"

- The speaker displays confidence.
- The speaker's voice is well orchestrated and modulated.
- Eye contact is maintained throughout.
- Visual Aids are designed and used as an aid for the AUDIENCE.
- If a 'script' is used it is written in "talk-writing" and shared NOT READ!
- Presentation is focused on what listener needs to know to 'buy in' to concrete ideas presented - not just on what you want to tell them.

**REMEMBER:**

All talks present information. The business world looks for guidance. *"What do we do with the information?"* It is your job to tell them. That is what a powerful presentation does!

# Road Map for Putting a Presentation Together
## or
# "THE ART OF TALKWRITING"

In this section you will go step by step through the process of imagineering your presentation. You will find reminders from other points we've made throughout this book. Here is where you *"get it all together"*.

## Starting the Process:

| | |
|---|---|
| a. | Know why you are talking. |
| b. | Know who you are talking to. |
| c. | Organize your talk to achieve (a) |

## Why?

Fill in this sentence:

**"When I have finished speaking I want my listener(s) to do . . . . . . . . . . . . . . . . . . . . . . . . . . . . . . . . . . . . . . . . . . . !"**

Then you are ready to ask:

**"What do I have to say to get action I want?"**

| |
|---|
| |
| |
| |

- **Do not try to develop ideas and organize them at the same time.**
  a. Brainstorming for ideas
  b. Hoe and weed
  c. Decide on format

- **Why a Format?**
  a. Helps you get started
  b. Links the units of your talk
  c. Keeps you on track
  d. Saves you time

## Ways to Brainstorm

 **"Key-word Listing", "Point-Listing", or "Clipping and pasting".**

The title doesn't matter. The point of the exercise is to help you put down ideas without writing sentences. **DO NOT START CREATING - YET!**

- Quickly list all the points you might want to cover. Do it rapidly. Simply scribble words and phrases.

- Do not try to organize or categorize at this point. Just let the ideas flow freely. Try to do it non-stop. Letting one idea trigger another.

- After a few minutes of this you will have a great many ideas. Look them over.

- Number them according to 'like' categories.

- Decide which is your central idea. Discard the rest.

- You now have a cluster of ideas around your central theme.

- Add any other ideas that fit this focus. Discard anything else. It is not useful to you here.

- When you're jotting down these ideas you should leave space between each idea. Sometimes easier to re-arrange on a desk then in the computer.

  - You can print them out, cut them into strips
  - One idea per strip, cut these strips and "play cards" with them
  - You simply stack them in 'like' categories
  - You can even re-arrange them

The whole focus of brainstorming is to let you generate ideas; hone them; feed them; but do not start trying to write a script! Remember it is easier to move, change, eliminate and add to an unfinished piece of writing.

## 2. "Mind Mapping", "Word Mapping", "Spiderwebbing", or "Clustering",

It has many names but they all refer to one method.

- **Start with a blank piece of paper.**
- **Draw a circle in the middle.**
- **Write your "topic" inside this circle.**

You now simply write down ideas as they come to you.

- As you get one idea - pursue it - circle each word or phrase and join them.

- As a new idea pops up - make a new circle joined to the centre one and go at it again.
- If you think of something else to add to a particular idea - just join it on.

When you've finished you will have all your ideas sorted out. You then choose the area(s) you want/need to concentrate on and work with them.

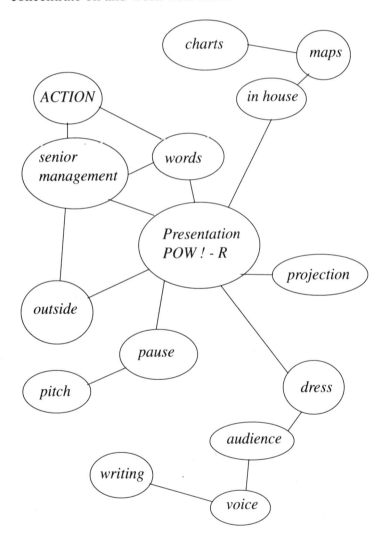

# A. Format for Organizing Talks

## Steps:

### 1. Start with your reason for speaking

## Examples:

- **Here's an opportunity**... I'm going to show you how to cash in on it.

- **We have this problem**... I will recommend etc

- **We can generate new business**(or spark existing)...let me share...

- **Our goal for this year is**........: here is a way you can reach that goal.

- **Real customer service is the key to success in our business**...I have looked at ....

- **Here is a way to move ahead of our competitors**...

(You've alerted listeners to the way you want them to listen to your talk: the action focus.)

### 2. What happens if we don't do this? or solve this?

Reach goal? develop this plan? adopt the strategy? (Identify consequences of no action; the problems they may encounter in trying to reach a goal; the way the problem, the need, or lack of goal is affecting business?

### 3. How you think they can solve

problem; reach goal; develop opportunity; improve quality; generate new business, move ahead etc.

### 4. How this will benefit the people you are speaking to.

### 5. Support ideas in logical order to get the results you want - give examples.

### 6. Summarize or review your proposal tying to its benefits for your listener(s)..

### 7. Ask for action and set deadline for this action.

## Remember:

All talks present information BUT your job is to direct your listeners. You show them how to use the information.

It is your responsibility to organize what you say properly. Only then can people follow you as you want them to do!

# B. Organizing your Talks

- **Logical order - some common examples:**

  1.  Chronological
  2.  Priorities
  3.  Compare/contrast
  4.  Familiar to unfamiliar
  5.  Problem/cause/solution (or vice versa!)
  6.  Advantages/disadvantages.

- **Find the right buttons to push.**

There are four basic drives motivating most people:

  1.  Pleasure
  2.  Survival
  3.  Egotism (concern for self)
  4.  Altruism (concern for others)

## Example:

- A salesperson may appeal to pleasure of ownership when planning a sales approach.

- You appeal to a superior's sense of survival when your talk focuses on ways to strengthen his position.

- You appeal to someone's ego when you suggest the proposed project will put person in the spotlight.

- You appeal to a persons sense of altruism by showing them how their action will truly help"ABC" in "DEF" ways.

# Suggestions To Get You Started

● **Use Anecdotes**

Just make sure they are relevant to your subject and the audience.

● **Try using a quotation that sets the stage**

In working with people on communication I often start with "You cannot change the wind; but you can adjust your sails!" It ties directly to adjusting your subject to your audience. It works for me.

One of my clients liked it so well he recently borrowed the phrase to open his talk on new directions for his company. It worked very well for him too!

● **You might try to involve your audience VERY quickly**

*(e.g.: "How many did . . . ?"; "What's at the top of your wish list"?)* Refer to members if you know them. Have them recall a common success or activity, etc.

● **Start with an attention getting statement**

Just make sure it is tied to your talk. If you just use a *"shock treatment"* it can backfire. Your listeners have been given permission to think about something else. You then have to pull them back to your topic.

● **You can make a promise**

*"In the next twenty minutes I will give you . . . "* (work from here on next time.)

# Suggestions To Get You Out

Always call for action in your closing remarks:

1. **Summarize:**

   These are the five ways...

2. **Anecdote:**

   "Even when you are falling on your face - you are moving ahead!"

3. **Ask a rhetorical question:**

   What will happen if....?

4. **Make a statement:**

   Take time to learn more.......

5. **End as you began:**

   Our customers are always right...

**How to Develop "AA"
Audience Appreciation**

# YOUR
# AUDIENCE

Keep your focus going outward.

"'**A**' is the first letter of the alphabet.
Let is stand for '**audience**'
your first consideration."

# SUCCESSFUL SPEAKERS HAVE
# THESE ABILITIES IN COMMON

1. **They care about the people they are talking to.**
   Only then will you establish a rapport. Think of people who have had a positive influence on your life, a college professor, a special supervisor. They cared and shared in a way that helped shape your life.

2. **They "connect" with their audience.**
   You can only do this if you have taken the time to know your audience. Without this vital knowledge your message may miss its mark.

3. **They understand the four basic drives motivating all of us.**
   Survival. Pleasure. Egotism. Altruism.

4. **They speak from a solid base of knowledge.**
   They use their own experiences and research as the basis for what they say. They do not speak when they have only third party knowledge. They do not set themselves up as sources of knowledge when theirs is limited.

5. **They remember that first letter in the alphabet - "A" for Audience.**
   You'll get an A from your audience if you keep them in mind at all stages of preparation and delivery.

Before you start putting a presentation together; before you respond to a question at a meeting; before you can successfully share your ideas - you must know to whom you are talking.

Ask yourself these three questions:

> 1. **Who am I talking to?**
>
> 2. **Will they be ready to listen?**
>
> 3. **How will they respond?**

At the end of this chapter you will find an audience analysis questionaire to help you get a handle on your audience. Not all questions will apply all the time, of course. But if you keep this handy in your *"Presentations File"* you will save yourself a lot of wasted work. You will also have yourself facing the right way to score the points you want.

Although the receiver of your message is part of the **P.R.E.P.** process, it is so crucial to success it must be considered as a separate *Key.* It is, perhaps the most important key of all!

## You want to achieve three things every time you face an audience:

1. **ACCEPTANCE**
2. **UNDERSTANDING**
3. **ACTION**

Most people only ask themselves *"What do I want to say?"* Of course this is crucial. But, you cannot know what you want to say, what you need to say, **UNTIL** you analyze your audience.

The information you share may be essentially the same. The way it is presented; the areas of emphasis; the focus; all depends on the **WHO** - your listener!

## Who are these people you want to listen to you?

- People you work with? Are they equals?
- More senior? More experienced?
  Less experienced?
- From your profession?
- People you want on your side?
  People who want you on their side?
- What do they know about your subject?
  More / as much as / less than you?
- Are you talking to friends? Strangers?
  Relatives?
- Are they older or younger?
- Potential customers? Buyers? Sellers?
- Do you want them to buy into a concept?
- Are you selling a product or a service?

These are some of the questions you must answer if you want your listeners to accept you **AND** act on your ideas.

Why do you need to do this homework? The answer is simple. To accomplish your goal. To be accepted, understood, **AND** get the action you want after you stop talking!

- **Whether you are talking to one person or one hundred and one people, identify your audience in relation to your message - if you want to be successful.**

# Here are a few points to keep in mind:

- **Experience/Knowledge**

  Your talk should build on your audience's previous knowledge of the subject. Don't bore people by repeating what they know. If you need to remind them of specifics, build that approach into the talk.

  On the other hand, don't cause confusion and disinterest by presuming they know more than they do!

- **Generalist/Specialist**

  Generalists will want ideas that are broader and more easily understood. Audience composition. Are you talking to men, women, both? What is the age of your listeners? What range can you expect? It can affect the examples you use to illustrate your ideas.

  Historical references understood by the 50-plus group could be lost on 30-year olds. Women are very sensitive about sexist comments. Ethnic comments will get you into hot water in a hurry.

- **How many**

  You can be more informal with a smaller group. The space you use and the way you use that space will be affected.

  A board room presentation will be handled differently from a speech in an auditorium. Selling to one person in an office requires one approach. Presenting and discussing projects in a small group setting needs another.

## ● Social/Political

You cannot impress an audience if your economic background talk is about something to which they simply can't identify.

Your job is to know your audience so well you can use examples, words, and situations within the parameters of their understanding.

What do they know about you? Do they know you are knowledgeable about your product or subject?

Has a *"reputation"* preceded you? Will you have to overcome antagonism or apathy?

If, for example, you are going to talk about weight and heart problems and you are overweight, how will you orchestrate your presentation to bridge this credibility gap?

Attitude towards subject - is your audience for, against, or neutral towards the topic you will discuss?

# Note:

1. You will not change your ideas through audience analysis. What you will do is decide if you need to adjust your approach to the way you will **PRESENT** your views.

2. Supporting data may have to be introduced in a different way or at a different stage in your presentation.

## Cooper Communicating Tool

● **You cannot always control the WHO - your listener.**

● **You CAN control the WHAT and the HOW**

These are the two factors that spell success or failure.

After you have analyzed your audience, you need to analyze the speaking situation.

## WILL THERE BE ANYONE ELSE SPEAKING?

● If you are part of a group making presentations to upper management , make sure you know what they will be saying. Know where you will be on the "program". The length of the other presentations.

● When possible, find out what other companies have been invited to submit proposals.

● If you are part of a panel, find out in advance who the other members are and where they stand. If you know one of the members is a top speaker with great presence, don't panic. Forewarned is forearmed. You will not try to be anyone but you. You will work at presenting yourself in an organized, honest, persuasive way.

● What is the occasion? Is it a weekly "catch-up-with-each-other" get together? A once a year opportunity to let the whole company know what your section is doing - all in twenty minutes?

● At a once a week get together you will have more flexibility. The presentation is likely be less formal. At the "once-a-year-let's-hear" opportunity you know time is limited so your focus must be tighter and clearer.

### Cooper Communicating Tool

● **When you speak always CONCENTRATE on your audience and what you want them to DO when you finish speaking!**

# AUDIENCE ANALYSIS GUIDE

## A. Who are they?

**1. How many people will be there?**

**2. Where do they come from?**

| | |
|---|---|
| Your Profession | _____ |
| Consumer/user Group | _____ |
| Your Dept. | _____ |
| Public | _____ |
| Company | _____ |
| Other | _____ |

**3. How many are familiar with subject**

| | |
|---|---|
| All | _____ |
| Half | _____ |
| Few | _____ |
| None | _____ |

**4. Why do they need this information?**

| | |
|---|---|
| They make decisions | _____ |
| They must be kept updated | _____ |
| They carry out decisions | _____ |
| Other | _____ |

**5. Why from you?**

| | |
|---|---|
| You want to present to this group | _____ |
| Your specialty | _____ |
| Other | _____ |

106

## 6. Will they be able to understand you or your message?

Background on subject limited     _____

Background on subject good     _____

Command of English limited     _____

Command of English good     _____

Will understand discipline's "jargon" _____

Will not understand "jargon"     _____

## Note:

● **Does your talk have enough/too much/ too little information needed to have listeners do what you want them to do?**
(keep checking this as you develop your presentation)

# B. Will they be ready to listen?

## 1. When are you speaking? Is your talk -

Just before or after a break     _____

The first     _____

Close to the end     _____

An obligatory event     _____

## 2. Will they have background ahead of time or with them that could distract?

Yes     _____

No     _____

Do not know     _____

3. **Will they view you -**

| | |
|---|---|
| As an expert | _____ |
| A stranger | _____ |
| A peer  to be taken seriously | _____ |
| Someone you can get info from anytime | _____ |

4. **Is there an event or activity in your audience's background you can tie to your talk to bridge any gap?**

| | |
|---|---|
| Yes | _____ |
| No | _____ |
| Have to think about it | _____ |

5. **Is there anything from your background you can use to help audience identify positively with you?**

| | |
|---|---|
| Yes | _____ |
| No | _____ |
| Have to think about it | _____ |

# C. How will they respond?

1. **What is the position of your audience now?**

| | |
|---|---|
| No opinion% | _____ |
| You don't know% | _____ |
| Agree% | _____ |
| Disagree% | _____ |

2. **What are your "worst case" disaster areas?**

_____

_____

3. **Can you clearly identify the most important benefit to the decision makers in your audience?**

| | |
|---|---|
| Need to think about it | _____ |
| Yes | _____ |
| No | _____ |

4. **Have you heard any audience members give a presentation? What support materials did they use?**

| | |
|---|---|
| Slides | _____ |
| Graphs | _____ |
| Examples | _____ |
| Personal Experiences | _____ |
| Stories | _____ |
| Other | _____ |

5. **Can you think of at least two challenging questions audience members might ask?**

1. _____

2. _____

6. **What follow through will you need?**

| | |
|---|---|
| Take-aways? | _____ |
| Copy of talk? | _____ |
| Further report? | _____ |
| Post-talk discussion? | _____ |
| Other | _____ |

KEY NO. 7

**Two more ways to focus
on speaking successfully**

# I's AND
# EYES

If you don't look at your listeners
why should they think you are
talking to them?

" You can see a lot just
by look around. "

**Yogi Berra**

To be effective as a speaker you must master your *I's* and *Eyes.*

Think of a large arrow pointing at you. This is created by you as you think about what you want to say.

Make the arrow curve back. Cross out the *I* and put **U** in instead.

It is as simple as that. Once you start thinking in terms of your audience, you will develop distinct change in your approach and your attitude.

Your message is no longer "Here's what I have to say". It becomes "Here's what you need to know - to do what you will want to do **AFTER** I have finished talking to you."

This switches you back to the **P.R.E.P. / T.R.I.M.** process very quickly.

It allows you to make a decision as to what course to take to help your listener make the right decision.

Let's look at the other **"EYES"**. The **"EYES"** you use to look at your audience.

● **You cannot share an idea if you don't look at the receiver of that idea.**

## You make Eye Contact because:

- ● You want feedback from your listener
- ● You want to remove the distance between you and your audience
- ● You really want to share an idea
- ● You want to 'touch' someone too far to reach

- **"Mouth open - eyes up !!!"**

## Note:

1.  **When you make eye contact ,You don't have to stare.**

    Simply give one thought to one person. Move along (in the pauses) to another part of the group; look that person in the eyes too.

2.  **If you have notes or a script BE CAREFUL.**

    Glance at your first idea; raise your eyes and share with your audience; pause while they digest that idea and you glance down at the next group of words that constitute an idea. This is why you have to learn to *Read Right!*

3.  **You must look at your listener..**

    If you want to make that person accept what you are saying.

- **Eye contact is just that! To succeed with your audience you must look at them.**

- **This rapport really strengthens your message. Your audience knows you are talking TO them not AT them.**

You have probably heard a few ideas for making "eye contact" easy.

- **Myth No. 1**

> *" Just think all your audience is sitting there naked. Then they won't bother you and you can look at them!"*

Nonsense! Why would you want to waste your energy and divert your concentration from your purpose. Think of your message. Think of the action you want from your audience. You will have no problem looking at them.

- **Myth No. 2**

> *" Look over their heads" or "Look to the corners of the room." or "Look between people when you are seated around a boardroom table".*

Your audience is not fooled. They know where you're looking. If you talk to the back wall some will turn to see who is sitting back there! Look past the eyes or look at another part of the listener's head and your listener may start wondering if the remains of luncheon is still on the left cheek!

- **Myth No. 3**

> *"Concentrate on the person or people who look disinterested. Win them - you win all!!!"*

Don't count on it. The disinterested person may never listen to you. Concentrate on those showing interest and attention. They will give you feedback. They will share the moment with you. Don't let someone who got up on the wrong side of the bed "rain on your parade".

114

**The Final Key**
**Ways to make it turn for you**

# PATIENCE
# AND
# PRACTICE

The ladder of success isn't climbed with your hands in your pockets.

> "You cannot learn to play the piano
> by leaning against it!"

Confidence for a woman can be putting on lipstick without a mirror. Confidence for a man can be shaving without a mirror.

Confidence in *speaking* comes from working with your speaking techniques until they are automatic. You cannot be worrying about whether you are projecting your voice while you are trying to project your ideas!

- **You need to spend quality time working with your voice so it is there for you - always!**

One of my sons was a ski racer. He didn't just do ski racing. He worked out every day, summer and winter. If he wasn't doing set exercises, he was bicycling so many miles a day to build muscles. He was running up and down hills, lifting weights, working on his skis and waxes and then writing down the pluses and minuses of each day's performance in his journal. A downhill ski race lasts less than three minutes - tops. The preparation goes on and on.

Apply the same scenario to speaking with **POW ! - R.** You are not preparing for a single talk but for a lifetime of challenges and successes.

Take a page from the stories of Olympic participants. The swimmers and divers whose grace makes what they do seem simple; the gymnasts who seem to float; the young skaters who thrill you with their expertise. They did not reach their level of excellence by simply *wanting* to achieve, they *worked* at it - every day.

- **You aren't looking to win the world's presentation championships. You are looking to influence others. To make what you say matter - to you and those who hear you.**

116

- **You are also asking others to invest an irreplacable commodity in you, their time.**

You owe it to your listeners as well as to yourself to speak effectively. This will make their investment and yours, worth it.

Spend as much time on your voice each day as you do getting your face ready to *"meet its public"* and I guarantee you'll be a speaker people will want to listen to! You will be amazed at how quickly you will have control.

There is no fairy godmother waiting to wave a magic wand. Wishing won't make it so. In the real world **YOU** hold this eighth key.

**Here are some ways you can work with your voice as you go about your normal day. Add to the list your own examples:**

- When you ar taking your daily shower don't just sing, practice counting up and down the scale.

- Instead of writing your own material, you can work on honing your speaking skills by using the works of other writers.

- _____
  _____

- _____
  _____

- _____
  _____

The following material will help you polish your Pow!-R-Speaking skills.

Use a pencil as you mark material. Then you can erase the marks if you don't like the rhythm or emphasis.

When you work with other material you can allow yourself to really free your voice. Overdo Shakespeare. ***Keep your spoken phrases short - six words at most.***

## Sample of how to space these out:

- *To every thing / there is a season, / and / a time to every purpose / under the heaven:*

- *Since / we have granted / all these things / for God, / for the better ordering / of our kingdom, / and / to allay the discord / that has arisen between us / and our barons,*

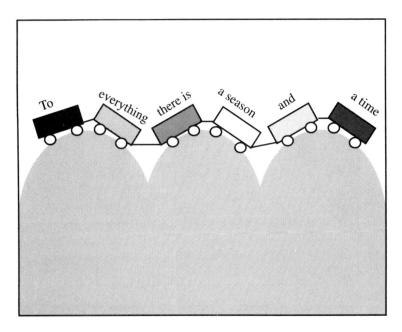

# PASSAGES FOR PRACTICE:

*To every thing there is a season, and a time to every purpose under the heaven:*

*A time to be born, and a time to die; a time to plant, and a time to pluck that which is planted;*

*A time to kill and a time to heal; a time to break down, and a time to build up;*

*A time to weep and a time to laugh; a time to mourn, and a time to dance;*

*A time to cast away stones, and a time to gather stones together; a time to embrace, and a time to refrain from embracing;*

*A time to get, and a time to lose; a time to keep, and a time to throw away;*

*A time to rend, and a time to sew; a time to keep silence, and a time to speak;*

*A time to love, and a time to hate; a time of war, and a time of peace.*

**Ecclesiastes**

Since we have granted all these things for God, for the better ordering of our kingdom, and to allay the discord that has arisen between us and our barons, and since we desire that they shall be enjoyed in their entirety, with lasting strength, for ever, we give and grant to the barons the following security.

The barons shall elect twenty-five of their number to keep, and cause to be observed with all their might, the peace and liberties granted and confirmed to them by this charter.

If we, our chief justice, our officials, or any of our servants offend in any respect against any man, or transgress any of the articles of the peace or of this security, and the offence is made known to four of the said twenty-five barons, they shall come to us - or in our absence from the kingdom to the chief justice - to declare it and claim immediate redress.

**from the Magna Carta 1215**

● **Present governments could learn a lesson from the short sharp writing here - couldn't they.**

Charles Dickens was not only a renowned writer, he was extremely popular as a reader of his writings. Here are some passages from his works. You will find they are written for talking.

● It was the best of times, it was the worst of times, it was the age of wisdom, it was the age of foolishness, it was the epoch of belief, it was the epoch of incredulity, it was the season of light, it was the season of Darkness, it was the spring of hope, it was the winter of despair, we had everything before us, we had nothing before us, we were all going direct to Heaven, we were all going direct to the other way - in short, the period was so far like the present period, that some of its noisiest authorities insisted on its being received, for good or evil, in the superlative degree of comparison only.

- There was a king with a large jaw and a queen with a plain face, on the throne of England; there was a king with a large jaw and a queen with a fair face, on the throne of France. In both countries it was clearer than crystal to the lords of the State preserves of loaves and fishes, that things in general were settled for ever.

**From A Tale of Two Cities - Charles Dickens**

- She was a fat old woman, this Mrs. Gamp, with a husky voice and a moist eye, which she had a remarkable power of turning up, and only showing the white of it. Having very little neck, it cost her some trouble to look over herself, if one may say so, at those to whom she talked.

- She wore a very rusty black gown, rather the worse for snuff, and a shawl and bonnet to correspond. In these dilapidated article of dress she had, on principle, arrayed herself, time out of mind, on such occasions as the present; for this at once expressed a decent amount of veneration for the deceased, and invited the next of kin to present her with a fresher suit of widow's weeds: an appeal so frequently successful, that the very fetch and ghost of Mrs. Gamp, bonnet and all, might be seen hanging up, at any hour in the day, in at least a dozen of the second-hand clothes shops about Holborn.

- The face of Mrs. Gamp - the nose in particular - was somewhat swollen, and it was difficult to enjoy her society without becoming conscious of the smell of spirits. Like most persons who have attained to a great eminence in their profession, she took hers very kindly; insomuch, that setting aside her natural predilections as a woman, she went to a lying-in or a laying-out with equal zest and relish.

**from Martin Chuzzelwit by Charles Dickens**

The following two passages from Shakespeare's Julius Caesar give excellent opportunities for increasing Vocal Variety:

In the first excerpt Brutus speaks. He has just helped kill Caesar. The citizens are condemning the act. Through his persuasiveness he turns them around. In fact he is so sure of himself he asks them to stay and listen to Mark Antony, Caesar's friend.

After Mark's speech the citizens turn against Brutus once again.

## BRUTUS :

- Romans, countrymen, and lovers!
  Hear me for my cause, and be silent
  that you may hear.

- Believe me for mine honour,
  And have respect to mine honour
  that you may believe.

- Censure me in your wisdom
  and awake your senses
  that you may the better judge me.

- If there be any in this assembly,
  any dear friend of Caesar's,
  to him I say  that Brutus' love to Caesar
  was no less than his.

- If then that friend demand
  why Brutus rose against Caesar,
  this is my answer:
  Not that I loved Caesar less,
  but, that I loved Rome more.

- Had you rather Caesar were living
  and die all slaves,
  than that Caesar were dead,
  to live all free men?

- As Caesar loved me,
  I weep for him;
  as he was fortunate, I rejoice at it;
  as he was valiant, I honour him:

- As he was ambitious - I slew him.

- There are tears for his love;
  joy for his fortune;
  honour for his valour;
  and death for his ambition.

- Who is here so base that would be a bondsman?
  If any, speak - for him have I offended.

- Who is here so vile that will not love
  this country?
  If any, speak, for him have I offended.

- I pause for reply.
  (Citizens cry out NONE, Brutus, NONE !)

- Then none have I offended.

- I have done no more to Caesar
  than you shall do to Brutus.

- The question of his death is enrolled
  in the capitol;

- His glory not extenuated,
  wherein he was worthy,

- Nor his offences enforced,
  for which he suffered death.

- Here comes his body,
  mourned by Mark Antony;
  who, though he had no hand in his death,
  shall receive the benefit of his dying,
  a place in the commonwealth;

- As which of you shall not?

- With this I depart,
  that, as I slew my best friend,
  for the good of Rome,
  I have the same dagger for myself,
  when it shall please my country
  to need my death.

- **Keep practicing. Try them all and pick your favourites.**

Here is Mark Anthony's speech. By breaking it up into thought trains you'll find his writing really easy to read.

You look down, grasp one lines; look up and then you can say it.

By using vocal variety in the repeated lines, you will be learning to develop pitch / pace/ pause to where it is automatic for you.

- Friends, Roman, countrymen,
  lend me your ears.

- I come to bury Caesar,
  not to praise him.
  The evil that men do
  lives after them:
  The good
  is oft interred with their bones;

- So let it be with Caesar.

- The noble Brutus has told you
  Caesar was ambitious.
  If it were so
  it was a grievous fault;
  And grievously has Caesar answered it.

- Here, under leave of Brutus and the rest
  - for Brutus is an honourable man -
  Come I to speak at Caesar's funeral.

- He was my friend.
  Faithful and just to me.

- But - Brutus says he was ambitious,
  And Brutus is an honourable man.

- He has brought many captives home to Rome,
  Whose ransoms
  did the general coffers fill;

- Did this in Caesar seem ambitious?

- When the poor have cried,
  Caesar has wept;
  Ambition should be made of stronger stuff.

- Yet - Brutus says he was ambitious
  And Brutus is an honourable man.

- You all did see
  that on the Lupercal
  I thrice presented him a kingly crown,

- Which he did thrice refuse.

- Was this ambition.

- Yet Brutus says he was ambitious,
  And sure he is an honourable man.

- I speak not to disprove
  what Brutus spoke,
  But, here I am to speak what I do know.

- You all did love him once,
  not without cause;
  What cause withholds you, then,
  to mourn for him?

## FROM:   THOMAS E. DEWEY SPEECH

- The President has said
  we have a rendezvous with destiny.

- We seem to be on our way
  towards a rendezvous with despair

- Let us turn away from that rendezvous
  and, let us start going
  in the other direction
  and, let us start now.

- The one ultimate unforgivable crime
  is to despair of the Republic.

- The one essential to the survival
  of the republic
  is to know it will survive

126

and will survive into a future
that is always larger -
always better.

- In every era for a century and a half
it has been doomed to death
by gloomy young theorists
and - by tired and hopeless elders.

- And history laughs at them
each time the dynamic forces
of a free republic - led by free men -
have given the lie to the defeatists
while the system of free economic enterprise
has marched onward,
sweeping the nation's increased population
to full employment - and -
over higher living standards.

## EXERCISE IN VOCAL VARIETY

If you want listeners to *'get the picture'* when you speak - you must see what you are talking about before you say it. This verse will help you do this.

Strive for contrast in tone as well as pitch. Tie emotion to your words. See a *'wet fish'*; mentally grasp a staff; hear a lark sing.

### COMPARISONS

- As wet as a fish - as dry as a bone;

- As live as a bird - as dead as a stone;

- As plump as a partridge - as poor as a rat;

- As strong as a horse - as weak as a cat;
- As hard as flint - as soft as a mole;
- As white as a lily - as black as coal;
- As plain as a staff - as rough as a bear;
- As tight as a drum - as free as the air;
- As heavy as lead - as light as a feather;
- As steady as time - uncertain as weather;
- As hot as an oven - as cold as a frog;
- As gay as a lark - as sick as a dog;
- As savage as tigers - as mild as a dove;
- As stiff as a poker - as limp as a glove;
- As blind as a bat - as deaf as a post;
- As cool as a cucumber - as warm as toast;
- As flat as a flounder - as round as a ball;
- As blunt as a hammer - as sharp as an awl;
- As brittle as glass - as tough as gristle;
- As neat as a pin - as clean as a whistle;
- As red as a rose - as square as a box;
- As bold as a thief - as sly as a fox.

Many comparisons older than time!
Perhaps you can think of some others that rhyme.

**Anonymous**

Perhaps you can think of some other comparisons that will help when you are talking to an audience. It is important to paint a picture in their mind and this comes with practice.

128

The following specimen speeches are for practice. See what kind of expression you can put into them. Breathe life into the words.

Only practice will make you believable and someone people want to listen to.

- Despite a great deal of writing on the subject, today's manager is no closer to understanding employee 'motivation' than his counterpart of 50 years ago. If anything, employee motivation is more of a problem now than it was in the early 1900s. This doesn't mean that the work of behavioral scientists has been counter-productive. Their efforts have given today's manager a better insight into motivation. What is does suggest is that advances in understanding motivation hasn't kept pace. They haven't kept pace with the rapid changes in employee attitudes . . . these changing attitudes mean that what motivates employees today is very different from what it was give ... ten ... thirty years ago.

- Negotiating a salary when interviewing for a new job takes some careful planning. Only planning will get you the best possible package. To plan carefully entails acquiring an understanding of compensation alternatives and salary ranges. You also have to know what your short term and long term goals are. You need to know when to discuss sazlary, and how to discuss it. To help you get the highest prices for your services, here are some general guidelines to follow. As you study the guidelines you need to keep your objectives in mind. If you don't you may find yourself accepting a job at less than you're worth. when this happens you become unhappy very quickly. The result - you're soon back in the job market.

Don't knock it - you need it!

STEP TWO

STEP ONE

# HARNESSING YOUR NERVOUS ENERGY

# What is your greatest fear?

Studies have been made; surveys taken; famous speakers quoted in numerous surveys in answer to this question.

- **85 TO 87% replied "FEAR OF SPEAKING IN FRONT OF PEOPLE".**

- **Fear of dying usually ranks sixth or seventh!**

You can experience this fear in a one-to-one talk. You find the words don't come out the way you want them to!

It will rear its ugly head when you present a prepared speech to an expectant audience!

There is no magical formula "to get rid of nerves". Or to be more precise - nervous energy. Nor do you want to.

No one ever won an Olympic gold medal without nerve power! What you have to learn to do is *harness your nervous energy*.

The formula to successfully do this is simple:

- Focus on what makes you nervous.Assess the problem properly . Don't think about "What makes me nervous". Think about what generates this "Fear of Speaking". Write all these fears down.

- Change the way you look at these stumbling blocks. Apply this new knowledge when you are speaking.

- Focus on correcting the problem.

Here are some typical answers I have received in my many seminars and workshops when I posed the question, *"What makes you afraid to speak in front of people?"*

| | |
|---|---|
| 1. | Might make a mistake |
| 2. | Audience might not be interested |
| 3. | Don't like talking in front of peers |
| 4. | Fear talking in front of strangers |
| 5. | Not sure of subject |
| 6. | Others in audience might know more about subject |
| 7. | Everybody's looking at me! |
| 8. | Might lose train of thought |
| 9. | People will see me blush (or shake) |
| 10. | Not used to speaking in front of a group |
| 11. | Might fail |

Let's look at each of these *'fears'* and how to re-direct them.

## 1. Might make a mistake

If this is one of your fears, do what I do. "Remember the Persian rug makers." They are renowned for their exquisite work. I remember reading that these masters of the art of weaving always weave a mistake into their work because only God is perfect!

Making a mistake is not a problem. It is how you handle the mistake when you make it. Everyone makes mistakes. People who never make mistakes are people who have never tried!

You won't find people like that at the top of the ladder of success in work or life!

- If you give incorrect information; correct yourself. People will love you for it.

- Remember most of the people listening to you also list "Speaking in front of others" as their greatest fear! If you carry on they know there is hope for them. They are not there to criticize - they are there to listen!

I remember adjudicating a Speech Arts festival a few years ago. A little eight year old girl presented a lovely version of the test poem. There was just one problem. She left out a verse. I knew it because I had a copy of the poem in front of me. Despite this, she gave the best presentation in the class. The poem flowed. I gave her first place.

There were some mutterings in the room. I forestalled most of them by saying, "Here is a fine example of a candidate carrying on despite leaving out a verse." This mistake did not hurt the presentation. She was concentrating so much on the overall message she still fully shared the intent of the poet.

Let me share a story told by the Manager of a company where I worked many years ago.

When he was Sales Manager an invoice went out under his signature. The amount doesn't matter so I'll give you approximations. The bill was for say $70,000.00. The secretary typed $7,000.00. The customer chose to pay only that amount. The president called him in. This Sales Manager expected to be fired.

Instead the President said, "We have just bought you $63,000.00 worth of experience."

That Sales Manager went overseas in the Second World War and rose to be a General. He came back to this Company afterwards. He was Manager when I knew him but rose to be President of the Company - the largest in the Commonwealth! He learned from his mistake. He was worth the investment. So are you!

Remember that when you are afraid of making a mistake. You are only human. It is acceptable. Correct yourself if necessary **THEN** go back to concentrating on the message you want to deliver.

## 2. Audience might not be interested

- Are you the Pied Piper enticing innocents to listen to you?

- Do you carry a lasso?

People listen for very selfish reasons. They hope there is something in what is being said that will make their job or their life more interesting, enjoyable, meaningful, easier, or whatever.

The audience knows what you are going to talk about. Or else, they know you by reputation and want to hear anything you have to say.

Unless you are seven years old, in your first concert, and your brothers, sisters, cousins, and grandparents have been coerced into being in the audience, your audience **IS** interested.

Concentrate on your listener and the action you want. Your brain only handles one BIG idea at a time!

## 3. Don't Like Talking In Front of Peers

You talk with them at coffee break or lunch time. Probably bowl with them too. Look at this as an advantage. You know them. You can analyze them as you prepare *because* they are people who work with you. You know, or can find out how much they know or need to know about your topic to take the action you want them to take. They can be your biggest supporters.

If there is someone in the group who might make you 'nervous' talk to them before hand. Make them part of the solution; not part of the problem.

"I know you want me to do a good job on this presentation. If you sit too close I know I'll lose my concentration. Will you sit near the back? Thanks."

"I need someone to listen to me as I go over my talk. I wonder if you have a few minutes?"

Fellow workers can be your best support group. Don't fear them - just focus on what you need to say to help them take the action needed.

## 4. Fear of talking in front of strangers

First - the people you talk to are not strangers. You may not have been "formally introduced" but you know them. You have done your **P.R.E.P.!**

You know, at least in general terms, who you are going to talk to. Knowing that you then know **HOW** to say **WHAT** you want to say. The message can always be the same. The way to organize the message always depends on the **WHO.**

Try to find out as much as possible about your audience:

- How many will be there?
- How much do they know?
- Do you need background? Pictures? Slides?
- How important to them is the knowledge you share.
- Do they know this?

Again, concentrating on your audience will give you the tools to prepare for a successful talk!

## 5. Not sure of subject

It is amazing how often people give this as a reason for being nervous. *If you don't know what you are talking about you should be nervous!*

### Cooper Communicating Tool

**Remember this adage:**

*"It is better to keep your mouth shut
and be thought a fool,
than to open it and prove the point!"*

It is your job to know what you are talking about. It is your job to do more than that.

As I have said before - and will say again - you talk for one reason. You want your listener to respond, to act.

You not only have to know your subject, you have to know what you want your audience to do with the information about that subject **AFTER** you stop talking. Keep this foremost in your planning and you will remain focused. You will also successfully share your ideas.

## 6. Others in audience might know more about subject

This often happens. It is especially true in company presentations. What you have to remember is *you* have been asked to speak or the audience has accepted your proposal to speak. *They want to hear what you have to say!*

Your best supporters are often people who know your subject as well or better than you. If you say something they agree with, you have confirmed their opinion. When you present alternatives, or share ideas from **YOUR** point of view, you give them something different to think about.

When you focus your research and voice on their area of expertise you give the listener your slant on the problem.Remember, you are presenting your ideas based on your work and research. If the other *'experts'* in the audience want to share their ideas, they will speak. If management wanted to hear from them instead of you they would have been asked.

## 7. Everybody's looking at me

Would you feel more comfortable if they all turned their backs? If they all looked at the floor or each other?

*Communicating is a face-to-face affair.* Look in your mirror. That is what your audience sees. If you don't like what they see, change it. Take a look at Step 4 - Non-verbal messages. **YOU ARE THE MESSAGE.**

## 8. Might lose train of thought

Have you ever gone to another room to get something then couldn't remember what it was? What did you do to help you remember? *That's right! You retraced your steps.*

The expression *"train of thought"* is used purposely. It is to remind you there is a thread that weaves through your message. To help you 'keep on track' planning is essential. That planning will include a road map. The essential ingredients to move you from start to conclusion.

You don't have to rely on just key words. Jot down phrases, draw pictures on a card. What ever it takes to give you *"sign posts"*. Where equipment is available, use visual aids to help you keep focused - help you remember.

Check with Step 6 - Platform Polish. It will give you guidelines on writing a full script, it that is what you need, and gives further suggestions on how to use slides, flip-charts, notes and how to handle handouts.

If you do go blank for a moment, here are a couple of ways to get back on track:

- You can always go back to another aspect of the material you have already covered. Stress its importance.

- Go into a little more depth. (You will always have more information than you can put into your talk. Here is a chance to slip it in! Keep a positive outlook.)

- Jump ahead to your next point. When your mind clears you can go back and insert any information left out. The world will not stop turning if you jump from point C to point E. The sun will still rise tomorrow even if you never remember point D!

Incidentally, if you do remember, don't be afraid to say something like *"one point I didn't stress"* or words to that effect.

***Blank spots are often the result of tension.*** One way to relieve tension is to momentarily become more tense.

- Tighten one hand into a fist for ten seconds. (You can casually put your hand behind your back as you do this.)

- Shift your weight to release tension.

## 9. People will see me blush (or shake)

If you are worrying about blushing, or knocking knees, or your pulsing heart, you are not thinking *"audience"*. Again I say, *think of the message not the messenger!*

Incidentally most people **DO NOT** notice a blush. At worst they may consider you *'flushed'* with enthusiasm!

The extra pounding of your heart is just your brain looking after you. The message goes *'there is a big job to be done here'* and the brain starts that adrenaline flowing. It is the *'rush'* that makes any performer give the extra push necessary to come out a winner. *Don't fight it - use it!*

## 10. Not used to speaking in front of a group

If this is a problem, think of your audience in the right way and the problem will disappear.

You do not talk to six or sixteen or six hundred people. You do not talk to a group. You talk to one person and another person and another person.

I worked for a number of years as a Television and Radio host and commentator. My audience was always in the thousands. But I never thought of them in that way. They were people I could relate to because they were interested in what I had to say. If they weren't, they flipped the switch.

I know this approach was successful. In the early days of television I was the host of a daily information program. In those days most people on local television were *"personalities"*. People would point to them, rush them for autographs. But not me! When I was out shopping or attending a local function, no one rushed up to me. Time and again the person in front or beside me would start to talk to me ask if they knew me. Not being too good with names, I'd assume they did.  Then suddenly the inevitable comment would come out, *"Oh, you don't know me do you! I just felt I knew you from the way you talk to me on your program!"*

I couldn't have wished for a better indication that my *'message'* was getting across.

You are used to talking one to one and to groups.  You do it every day.  Every time you open your mouth you are giving a speech.  Be yourself.  Be totally committed to your message.  Concentrate there. People **WILL** listen and react positively.

## 11. Might fail

The only people who are failures in life are those who never learned  from mistakes.

> *" The only people who have never failed are those who have never tried!"*

- **If you have done your preparation properly (yourself and your message).**

- **If you put your heart into your preparation and delivery.**

You have not failed. You may not always reach the goal you want every time.  But the magic is there. There will be other opportunities to *'state your case'* and you'll do it better next time.

When I was first appointed Daily Commentary for the Canadian Broadcasting Corporation, I was worried that I would not be able to deliver top calibre commentaries every day.

Dorothea Cox, a very wise woman and the person who hired me, gave me this advice. I share it with you. I have silently thanked Dorothea many times in my career. I now do so publicly.

> *"Look at the top baseball players. They don't bat a thousand. Just try to establish the best batting average you can. If you do that all your work will be good - and some will be superb."*

- **You may have your own special 'fear' to add to the list. Treat it in the same way .**

- **Look at your "problem" and get rid of it.**

The other side of speaking

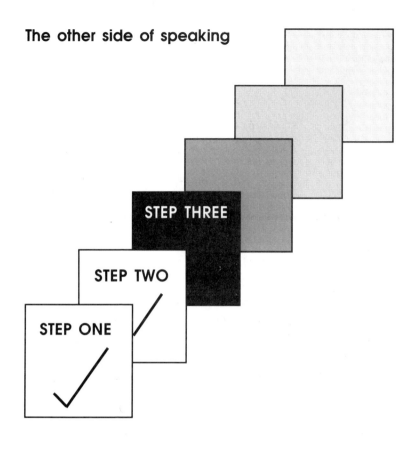

STEP THREE

STEP TWO

STEP ONE

# LISTENING
# EFFECTIVELY

> *"I know*
> *you believe*
> *you understand*
> *what you think I said,*
> *but, I am not sure you realize that*
> *what you heard is not*
> *what I meant."*

Listening is a vital part of communicating. We spend at least 50 percent of our communication time listening.

To be an effective speaker you must be a committed listener. **HOW DO YOU LISTEN?**

To paraphrase a comment by a former president of the United States *"You cannot listen yourself out of a job!"*

**B U T !!!** You can certainly talk yourself out of one if you don't polish your listening skills.

- **Listening is more than hearing**

  Listening is not only sensing a message, it is interpreting that message. You have to analyze the message so you can respond effectively.

- **Listening is a complicated process**

  Knowing how to listen can double the efficiency of business. Through the process of listening we receive and assign meaning to the sounds and words we hear.

  We must evaluate, appreciate, understand, classify or associate ideas. Only when we listen effectively can we get involved in effective problem solving; respond to new challenges and ideas; bolster a point of view; be effective as a speaker!

- ## Listening gives you a great deal of information

  Not just by what is said but the way it is said. We get most of our information today through our ears. This is not the generation of readers.

- ## Listening gives you the opportunity to analyze and evaluate information and data

  As you listen you can compare what you are hearing with other information you already have.

- ## Listening can introduce you to new ideas, new concepts

  It can help you as a speaker. The more you know the more effective you will be when you speak.

- ## Listen selfishly. "What is in this for me?"

  You are always a winner when you listen positively. Aside from simple politeness and respect for the speaker, think of these advantages.

  You can gain new information and ideas. You will have an opportunity to better understand the people with whom you are dealing. A big plus for you.

  People recognize the *'listener'*. You will find the courtesy reciprocated. They will really listen to you when you speak.

- ## Everyone likes to talk. Few people really listen.

  They *hear* words but do not *listen* to the ideas behind them. Too often they translate them into what they think the speaker said.

## Test Yourself:

Take a blank sheet of letter-size paper. Get a pen or pencil ready to write down some letters. Don't shortchange yourself by reading ahead!

When you write these letters spread them evenly across the top of the page. About an inch apart. You will be writing six letters in total:

- The first letter I want you to write is "S".
- Next write the letter "T".
- The next letter to write is "U".
- Move along another inch and write "P".
- The word is becoming clear now as you write "I".
- The last letter I want you to write is "D".

You have written the word **"S T U P I D"**. Or have you? Did you print the letters? Most people will print even though the word *'write'* is there nine times. Some people excuse this behaviour by saying *"I print when I write."*

My reply: *"you are taught to print and eventually you are taught to write. Your writing may be rather like printing, but it is called writing."*

I hasten to add that no one doing this test is stupid. Many are lazy listeners or in this case readers. Many people assume they know what you are going to say and stop listening to do what they think you want.

There is the other side to this communication gap of course. You must be very clear. If you had been asked to **"PRINT,** *do not* **WRITE,** *the following letters"* there would have been no mistaking the purpose.

Too often we presume we know what someone is saying or going to say. Right away we start preparing our retort. That response will often be based on insufficient information because the *'listener'* has not listened.

- **Do you like being interrupted when you are talking? I'm sure you don't. This is considered the number one annoying habit by nearly ninety percent of the public.**

This habit of interrupting grows out of the habit of not listening. Most people are so busy thinking about what they are going to reply to the first comment, they never listen to the rest of the argument.

Statements can become arguments as the speaker feels obliged to say, *"Just let me finish will you!"*

## For example, picture this:

| | |
|---|---|
| **Scene:** | An Office(might even be yours!) |
| **Players:** | Mary Jones and Chester Brown |
| **Background:** | There has been a discussion about buying a new telephone answering system. Mary had suggested a particular system. It was agreed it was the best one. However, Chester, the Office Manager, felt the price was too high. Mary had tried to point out the better system was worth the price. She lost the argument. |

A week later a competing company, carrying the same system, offers it to her at a price she knows Chester will accept. Excitedly she rushes into his office.

| | |
|---|---|
| **Mary:** | Chester, you know that telephone system you thought was too high priced, well...... |
| **Chester:** | (Interrupting) Mary, I haven't time to go through all that again. I told you..... |

| Mary: | (Interrupting) Wait a minute, you haven't heard what I have to say. I've been talking to Acme Supplies and..... |
|---|---|
| Chester: | (Interrupting) You've been doing what! After I made it clear we can't afford it you have the nerve to go over my head...... And so on!!!! |

Chester didn't give Mary a chance, but Mary was at fault too. She should have set up her message so that Chester would be ready to listen.

It is easy to listen *"with half an ear"* as the saying goes. This happens when you hear part of the message and feel you can write the rest of the script yourself. Usually you are wrong.

To be a better listener you need to think of what annoys you when you are speaking. People give out nonverbal messages of inattention. Here are few habits to avoid.

- Signing letters and memos when someone is talking.
- Answering telephone in the middle of a discussion.
- Saying "I was just on my way out but do sit down."
- Toying with a pen, paper clip or anything else on the desk.
- Not looking at speakers when they are talking.
- Trying to read something on the desk while person talks
- Interrupting to inject own ideas before person is finished.
- Looking like you're just waiting to 'jump in'.
- Facial expression never changes.
- Staring at speaker so as to intimidate.
- Sorting or signing then saying "Go on, I'm listening".

All these attitudes relay one message - you are not really listening.

You now know many of the reasons why you need to listen effectively. Why doesn't it happen?

## 1. Competition for attention

The telephone call you try to ignore may be more important. The letters and memos have to be signed. The stack of reports on your desk signals what you have to do as soon as you have finished speaking with the person in your office. You can hear raised voices somewhere. Are you needed elsewhere to moderate. These and many other distractions lead to the next problem.

## 2. Failure to concentrate

We live in a time where there is so much to distract us we have developed the ability to ''tune out'. You don't like the start of a TV show you switch channels. The buzz of the office machinery can irritate. You tune out that sound. You find the speaker's voice irritating to listen to so you don't. When concentration wanes, another problem emerges.

## 3. Emotions interfere

The way someone sounds - the inflection or emphasis can trigger an emotional reaction. The impulse is to talk - not to listen. Sometimes this emotional reaction prevents us from listening to what is being said. There are other feelings that can short circuit effective listening. The way someone dresses, an accent that takes real listening to understand, and many other factors. Whatever the cause, once emotions start getting in the way objective listening can be lost. That is the fourth reason for poor listening skills.

Instead of sitting up listeners tend to relax too much. Note taking is not organized effectively. There is a difference between speaking speeds and listening speeds. Instead of taking advantage of this by jotting down facts and ideas many people let their minds drift to other areas.

● **To listen effectively you must listen for facts and for the unspoken messages.**

# SOME GUIDELINES
# TO EFFECTIVE LISTENING

| THE KEY | POOR LISTENER | GOOD LISTENER |
| --- | --- | --- |
| Find area of interest | Tune out dry subjects. | Views speaker's comments as opportunity to learn |
| Judge content not delivery | Tunes out if delivery is poor. | Listens past inadequate delivery |
| Hold your fire | Tends to interrupt or enter into discussion before speaker is finished. | Doesn't get emotionally involved or judge until speaker is finished |
| Listen for ideas | Listens for facts only. | Listens for reasons behind facts. Listen for feelings. |

| | | |
|---|---|---|
| Resists distractions | Allows attention to wander. | Fights or avoids distraction, tolerates bad habits, concentrates on what is said. |
| Keep an open mind | Permits personal prejudices to get in the way. | Interprets from contents, listens actively to ideas - not the source. |
| Capitalize on fact thought is faster than speech | Tends to daydream with slower speakers. | Listens between the lines to tone; uses pauses to weight comments, make notes, summarize. |
| Exercise your mind | Resists difficult material, seeks light material. | Uses complex material as an exercise in understanding and growth. Ask for clarification when needed. |
| Work at listening | Shows little or no effort to understand. Too quick to say "What do you mean?" | Works hard at listening. Body language reflects active listening. |
| Be flexible | Makes no effort to adapt listening to speaker's way of organizing presentation. | Looks for central idea and organizational pattern. Takes concise, effective written notes to help keep message clear. |

Speakers need to study listener habits too!

The longer your message; the more fragmented the focus; the surer you can be your listeners will turn you off.

Speakers often make presumptions about the people they are talking to - don't fall into that trap.

Do not presume that just because your listeners are looking at you do not presume they are listening. *Look for signs of life!*

Are they nodding in approval? Raising an eyebrow? Smiling? Frowning? Sitting forward to *'catch every word'?*

When in doubt - get them involved. Ask for a show of hands if you need to. Change your position. Bring up that visual aid you've been saving.

To avoid this concern go back to *"Know your audience"* next time you prepare.

Make sure you are orchestrating your message and your voice to get the results you want - always.

Poor listening skills show up most vividly in one-to-one communicating.

Make sure you aren't guilty of these poor listening actions:

● **Do you often finish sentences when someone pauses for a moment?**

The pause is usually there to give you a chance to digest what has been said.

If you jump in you are demonstrating your inability to listen effectively before responding.

● **Do you "um-hum" a lot when someone is speaking to you?**

This can be very disturbing to the speaker. A nod of the head is just as effective.

152

- **Do you sometimes ask a question that has just been asked and answered?**

  A quick way to join the growing ranks of people building reputations as ego-centrics. They only listen to their own voices. And pretty soon the favour is returned - no one listens to them.

- **Do you start answering what you think is the question before the speakers is finished?**

  You have joined the ranks of the *"One-Person-Show"*. Today's business world has no place for the solo person who is only interested in self-generated, ego-centred thoughts.

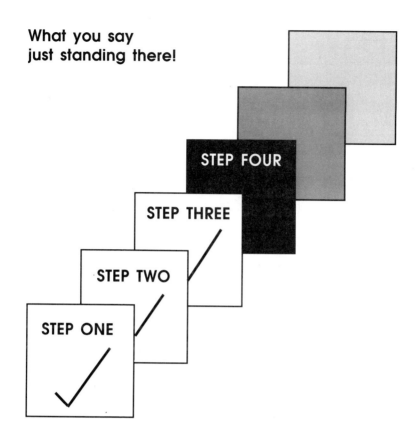

**What you say
just standing there!**

STEP FOUR

STEP THREE

STEP TWO

STEP ONE

# NON-VERBAL
# MESSAGES

> *"Every little movement has a meaning*
> *all it's own"*
>
> from an old song

Every day you see people, meet people, greet people. Before you say one word you transmit impressions, favourable or not, in a number of ways.

# Here's how you send non-verbal messages

## 1. Your Walk

- Is it slow, fast, listless, confident, hesitant, defiant, determined?

- Do you stride, saunter, strut, shuffle, stalk?

- What are you trying to convey to the onlooker? Walk it.

## 2. Your Posture

- Do you slump, stand like a drill sergeant, shift your weight from leg to leg as you talk, fold your hand across your chest, lean against anything handy?

- Next time you are in a group take a glance around the room. How many people are putting their best foot forward?

## 3. Your Clothes

- Are the clothes you wear always suited to the occasion? Not to casual or formal?

- Are you clean, neat, sloppy, too flashy, colours clashing? There is a saying "clothes make the person". That may not be true, but it certainly helps. A business suit is still the best investment for anyone in business.

## 4. Your Comestics

- If you are a woman - is your make-up suitable for the time of day or occasion?

- Is the perfume correct for occasion, your hair spray odourless or understated?

- If you are a man - is the cologne or aftershave lotion suitable or to overwhelming?

- Is your moustache or beard trim or shaggy?

- Being understated and simple but still elegant and stylish; ie. less is more.

## 5. Other Considerations

- It isn't fashionable to share the odour of "good honest sweat" or perspiration. Garlic toast or onion sandwiches don't go with one-to -one conversations.

- Clothes that are crisp, pressed and fresh, not ones that look like you just ran 10 miles in a rainstorm before talking and giving your presentation.

**DO YOU?**

- fuss with your hair,
- shake hands limply,
- clear your throat before you answer any questions,
- jingle the change in your pocket,
- play with the paper clip which held your notes,
- hold a pencil or pen in your hand?

**DON'T!!**

- **Avoid these negative non-verbal language like the plague!**

# Positive Non-Verbal Messages

- **GESTURES**

These often take the place of words. A shrug of the shoulders, a nod of the head, or a shake, is often all you need to get your idea across!

*"What do I do with my hands?"* A universal cry. Don't worry about them. Concentrate on what you are sharing with your listeners. If you gesture, it will come as a natural movement. You will give people visual endorsement of what you are saying.

You **CAN** put your hands in your pocket if you want to at some point in your talk. Just make sure you don't have keys or coins there. Don't leave facial tissues in your pocket either. You will end up shredding it and your audience can be distracted by the movement.

Unfortunately gestures are often executed simply for the sake of gesturing. Don't listen to people who say it adds vigour to your talk. More often it is simply distracting your listener from the message. It is hard enough to keep people interested. Don't turn them off by using phony gestures.

At the same time, do not feel you have to let your hands hang limply by your sides.

**THE BEST RULE TO FOLLOW:** A gesture should amplify or clarify the message. *"If it does - use it.* If it does not - forget it.

● **FACIAL EXPRESSIONS**

Approximately seventy percent of your non-verbal message comes from your face! Your face contains your mouth. So that is where people are going to look when you talk.

**DO NOT PUT YOUR FACE INTO NEUTRAL** to avoid over active facial expressions.

If you have been taught to keep a *'poker face'* - forget that lesson!

If you truly want to relate to your listener in an honest and meaningful way, don't play games. You have to be totally committed to your message if you want your listener to totally commit to your ideas.

If you have kept your face passive up to now, you need to work your  facial muscles. Here is a good way to start. Look at yourself in a mirror. Think of an emotion and say it with your voice and face as you utter **"NO"** or **"STOP"** or **"YES"** or **"OH"**.

**Example:**  Feel sad, surprised, angry, doubtful, happy fearful, bored.  After using the single word to help you focus on an emotion.  Then *"say it without words"*.

## ● HANDSHAKES

Handshakes can reveal a great deal about you.  A limp shake sends a *'limp person'* message.  Too firm a grip sends a *'domineering person'* message.  Try to find the middle ground. Grasp the person's hand firmly.  Despite the name you do not have to shake it vigorously!  Take a lesson from Queen Elizabeth, Prince Charles and Princess Diana, and other dignitaries who shake thousands of hands in a year.  A two second firm grasp sends positive vibrations.

## ● HOLD YOUR HEAD HIGH

Do you *'lead with your chin'?* You have to fight gravity all the time.  Try putting a small book on the top of your head and walking around.  A standard exercise at one time for developing good posture. It is still useful today.

When you let your head lead the way you start a chain of slumping.  Your shoulders roll forward; your arms swing forward slightly; your power base is squashed as the ribs sink down; your weight shifts; your stomach protrudes; your energy erodes through the soles of your feet!

**TRY THIS:**  Roll your shoulders in small circles towards your back.  Move your extended arms so your middle finger is in line with the side seam of your pants or skirt.  Feel the body begin to assume its proper *PowerTalk position*.  As an added bonus you will look as though you've just lost ten pounds around the middle!  You will also release tension form your neck and shoulder muscles.  An essential ingredient in speaking effectively.

By making sure you are not using negative or inappropriate body language and by developing positive body images you can present yourself more effectively.

Keep this upright position when you sit too. If you try to round your back to fit a chair you can add ten years to your looks. Try it. Sit and slump in front of a mirror. Men will find their suit collars look too big; their ties flop over to reveal too tight buttons on their shirts. Women look as if they have suddenly acquired a middle age spread; the shoulders look slumped with burdens' chins can double; waists expands noticeably.

Sit so your feet can be firmly placed on the floor. Try crossing your legs below the knees. If you are a woman and wearing an *'above the knee' skirt*, this is essential.

- **Look right**

- **Sit right**

- **Walk right**

- **Put your best foot forward to BE RIGHT!**

Sharing your words

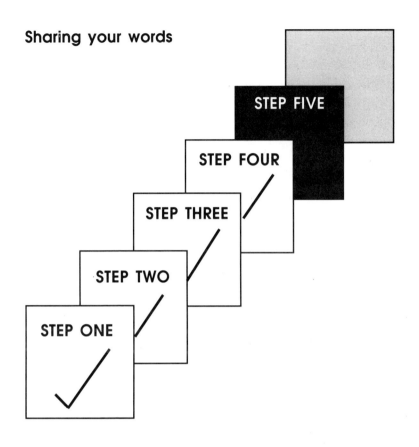

STEP FIVE

STEP FOUR

STEP THREE

STEP TWO

STEP ONE

READ
RIGHT

Effective presenters make eye contact. Easy enough to do when you are speaking *'off the cuff'* or from a skeleton Road Map.

In the real world many people do not have the time, or do not take the time, to become familiar enough with the material to go without a full script. Even with notes speakers often find themselves looking at the notes instead of the audience. This book gives you many positive ways to achieve *'Road Map'* status quickly. But, in the meantime how do you keep eye contact and read at the same time.

# Here's How to Read Effectively

Reading aloud means more than simply saying each word and saying it correctly. It means sharing information with your listeners. Sharing it in a way they can easily understand so they act and react the way you want them to.

## 1. Physical preparation

This means proper breath support and control. Have your breath *'at the ready'!*

Don't fall into the trap *"Take a couple of deep breaths - that will relax you"*. It's fine to take in a breath - but most people release the breath, then start to talk **WITH NO SUPPORT.** Take in a deep breath, and let it out slowly to help you relax, if it helps. **THEN TOP UP YOUR BREATH AGAIN SO YOU HAVE THE POW ! - R YOU NEED.**

## 2. Read the way you Pow !-R-Talk - in IDEAS

Just a reminder - Ideas are spoken phrases. A word or group of words uttered on one impulse of breath to transmit a single idea.

### 3. Remember: WHEN YOUR MOUTH IS OPEN - YOUR EYES ARE UP.

Remember Key 7. You can't communicate looking at a paper!

### 4. Use Key 4 - The four P's

Keep your spoken phrases short. New phrase = new pitch, pace and a pause.

Project needs special mention. Keep voice strong through the last word of a phrase. If you start looking at your paper for the next phrase, your voice will be restricted, your focus divided, your impact lessened.

### 5. Within your phrases look for the important word

This carries the essence or central theme of your talk. Ex: by the **SIDE** of the road or By the side of the **ROAD**. *Your meaning changes with your emphasis.*

### 6. Mark your script for easy interpretation

Don't assume you'll remember the way you want to say it. You will be too busy and involved. Here are some suggested marks you can use:

| | | |
|---|---|---|
| / | - | Pause to indicate end of idea. |
| // | - | Longer pause. |
| O | - | Circle important word. Don't underline |

When you read your eyes will slide by an underlined word. Put a circle around the world and it acts like a Bull's-eye. You can't miss it.

## 7. As you move through your material look for the NEW IDEA

Think of the new ideas as a word or words that modify, clarify and/or amplify former information. By use of the word/new idea the meaning is subtly changed.

Ex: The bank showed and interest in the site. The interest was heightened when the new figures were released. These new figures reflected a healthier economy.

## 8. Remember - just reading without making any mistakes is not enough!

You have to give clear signals by the way you phrase, emphasize, use pitch, pace, volume, and modulation.

## 9. Preparing your material

Make it easy on yourself if you are going to read from a prepared script. Check the examples at the end of this chapter.

- Keep typed lines short and to one side. This allows space to put in references and notes. (Example shown in Key 8.)

- Always have material typewritten. Use larger print especially if wear eye glasses. I always have my material printed large enough for me to read if my glasses are misplaced!

- Never use more than 2/3's of a page. Your eyes do not have to travel as far down the page. Your voice doesn't get 'squashed'.

- Never have half an idea on one line and the rest on the next line or next page. Your thought process will be interrupted. Your delivery won't flow, it will be jumpy.

## 10. Lastly - and most important, keep your voice energized and flexible

It is just too easy to slip into poor communicating habits such as mumbling, muttering, and monotone delivery.

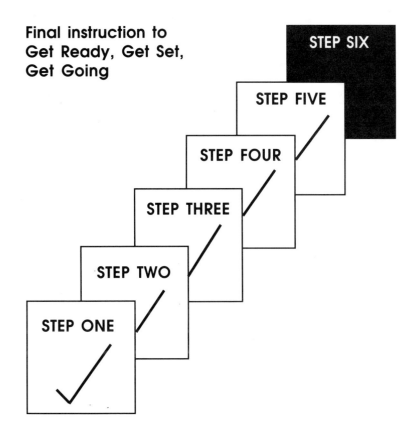

**Final instruction to Get Ready, Get Set, Get Going**

STEP SIX

STEP FIVE

STEP FOUR

STEP THREE

STEP TWO

STEP ONE

# PLATFORM POLISH

# Powerful Presentation Reminders

- Always tie the presentation to benefits for the listener
- Create through ideas not paragraphs
- Be organized, complete, concise
- Show your audience you are properly prepared
- Start out with a "road map"
- Follow the map - enthusiastically

Why do so many presentations fail or fall short of expectations?

- Not focused on action wanted
- Poorly constructed
- Written in too long sentences and paragraphs

Abraham Lincoln used to say he liked a talk "to be as personal and familiar as a chat between two people riding along on a buckboard".

This is still good advice. Whether your listeners number three or three hundred you must **TALK** to them not at them. That is why you prepare a *"talk" not a "speech"*.

## Cooper Communicating Tool

- **Your presentation must reach an audience tuned to station "WII-FM" = "What's In It For Me?"**

**FOCUS** on your audience and on what you want them to do when you've finished talking. This focus will guide you. It will show you:

- What you need to put in AND leave out!
- What language you will use.
- The logical order you must follow.
- What visual aids you need.

**REMEMBER** the first twenty words are more important than the next twenty thousand. This is where the audience *'buys in'*.

## Cooper Communicating Tool

- **You ALWAYS know what you want to say.(If you don't, keep quiet!)**

- **What you work on is - HOW TO SAY IT to get  what you want!**

# Overall Organization

Keep the **PRESENTATION** separate from the *"Thank you for having me here"* part. The latter is said in a polite but off-hand way - if possible physically separated from your *"Stage"*...if only by a half-step.

**Organization will:**

- Say what you're going to say
- Say it
- Say what you said

Everything you say - everything you demonstrate will be geared to your purpose.

# Starting the Process of Presentation Preparation

1. **Know why you are talking.**
2. **Know who you are talking to.**
3. **Organize your talk to achieve Step One.**

### STEP ONE: The why?

You must focus on the results you want - not just on what you want to say! First and always complete this sentence:

- **"When I have finished speaking I want my listener(s) to do.......!"**

Next - ask:

- **"What do I have to say/do to get the action I want?"**

172

## Example:

You are giving a talk on new developments in your organization. First ask *"Why is this information useful to my listener?"*

It isn't enough for them to go away knowing work is going on. You must also tie in *"This is important to you because...."* The "because" is your agenda. The reason you are speaking. It is the *"What you want them to do with the information you share with them."*

To do this properly you need to now the person or people you are talking to. This is the next step.

## STEP TWO: Analyze your audience

The more you know about the audience the more you can zero in on their needs. There are many questions you can ask yourself. Use the check list in Key 6.

- Where are they from? Within or outside your business area?
- How do they feel about your subject now?
- Do they know anything about it?
- What do they need to know to do; what do you want them to do?
- Age? education? from a different country?
- Will they REALLY be in a listening mode? (time talk takes place can be vital)
- What follow-up must you be ready for? Question period?
- How much change can you reasonably expect to make through your talk?

When you have answered these and any other special questions about your audience you harness their needs to yours. Do this by touching the right buttons.

Most people agree there are four basic drives that motivate people: survival; pleasure, egotism (concern for self) and altruism (concern for others). Fit your purpose into one of these areas. Sometimes you have to push all of them!

## Examples:

- You will appeal to a superior's sense of survival when your report shows how his position is strengthened.

- A salesperson may use appeals to pleasure in planning a sales approach.

- You appeal to someone's ego when you suggest volunteering will give them a sense of pride.

- You appeal to someone's altruism by letting them know what they do will help others live better; longer; more peacefully; with improved health; and so on.

## STEP THREE: Organizing and writing your talk.

## Remember:

Most people start by sitting down and starting to write the talk - starting with the introduction. *Don't do this.*

Do some *"freewheel thinking"*.

**MINDMAP** or random list. Get your ideas - **ALL** your ideas - written down..

---

- Write the thoughts down as they occur.
- Do this non-stop.
- Do not try to organize and generate your ideas at the same time!

---

After about ten minutes of non-stop idea planting you are usually ready to *'trim down'*. Read over your thoughts.

If you have used the MindMapping technique, check various categories. Flesh out or cut out as you group and support like areas. Try to keep to three or four categories.

If you have jotted down a list of ideas on your computer, a printout is essential at this stage.

You need to have all your ideas visible. Number them according to areas.

To keep the thought process positive you might try actually using your scissors to cut out each idea and stacking into appropriate piles. *You are organizing your talk without any rewriting!*

Using them like stacks of cards you can arrange, re-arrange, add to, or discard. You can take these pieces of paper and paste your ideas on another sheet of paper - leaving spaces between for additional thoughts.

Using either method, in a very few minutes you have the essence of your talk. Probably within twenty minutes! You will hang your talk on this skeleton. The basic structure is directed and lean. Any further research needed to flesh it out is clearly defined.

- You are on target
- You know what you are going to say
- You know how you are going to say it because you know your audience
- You know what you want them to do when you have finished talking

You now have the body: *"The Message"*, but you aren't through yet.

*You can now write your conclusion.* How often have you heard a speaker comes to the end of a talk and just stop.

# Some overall comments

- At all stages of your talk watch your language.

- Avoid the abstract.

- Keep words concrete.

- Remember Winston Churchill's advice - "Never use a pound word when a penny one will do!"

- Use simple sentences. This means avoiding dependent clauses.

- Paint pictures. Your words have to send out clear images.

- People will not buy into unfocused ideas.

Some of these suggestions are essential in any part of your talk. They are particularly important as you begin. This is when you *'set your stage'.*

## Order of Writing:

1. **Body First**
2. **Conclusion**
3. **Introduction**

When you work from the action you want your conclusion is almost written for you. Your closing remarks will "say what you said" in a condensed manner. You will then call for the action you want.

This the "wrap". Where you stop and your listeners take over! If you've done your job well they will have digested the special knowledge you shared. They will be ready to act! *There are numerous ways to conclude.*

- Simply summarize the "up to now" information

- Use an illustration to underline points

- Call for **ACTION** (most conclusions do this)

- Use a quotation for an example of prose of poetry reflecting your ideas

Do not make it too long. Try not to conclude with *"In conclusion...."*. There are better ways. Here are a few ideas:

A simple pause will signal the *"beginning of the end"*. A shift in body position does the same thing. Here are some phrases to start you thinking in a different direction.

- "So, where does that leave you?"

- "Where do you really fit into this picture?"

- "The most important aspect you need to take with you is...."

- As my favourite teacher once said......."

- "Not everyone you meet will be ready for this challenge. BUT..."

The trick is to signal subtly. Tie it to your audience; ie it to your experience where possible. You gain added credibility.

- Your conclusion contains your action message.

- These are the last words your listener hears.

- You must have a motivated ending to give your listener a sense of purpose; a sense of completeness.

- There must be no mistake ; your listener now has the ball.

- If you do not plan your conclusion, you will not get the action you want. Your audience may not even realize you are finished!

**Now you can write "THE INTRODUCTION".** You cannot write a *"grabber"* introduction until you have planned your talk can you? The introduction is most important part of your talk.

- It sets you up.
- It sets your audience's attitude.
- It show them how they should listen
- It point out what they should listen for
- It indicates where you will go together
- It usually says how long the 'journey' will be.
- It allows you to alert your audience to the road map you have designed.

Because it is so important, and because it must tie in with your talk it **MUST** be written last.

Remember - the first fifteen or twenty words you say are more important than the next twenty thousand. The words and the way you say them will cause people to turn on to you or turn you off.

# Remember
# You can start your talk
# in many ways

Some people suggest *"Always start with a joke!"*

Humour is certainly useful in any presentation. As the song suggest, *"A spoonful of sugar helps the medicine go down!"* Just make sure it is indeed humorous **AND** is tied to your topic! It shouldn't be necessary to add - make sure it is in good taste.

Unfortunately there are still some people who think the way to make a point humorous is to make someone the "butt". **DON'T!**

# Presenting

Do not read your introduction! There is nothing wrong with having a script. Just make sure you are lifting the words off the paper.

Start watching speakers. You'll find more than half of them even keep their eyes on the speech as they tell you what they are gong to talk about.

I've even seen people look at their paper when they were saying, *"As President of this organization..."* or *"I'm really excited about this project...."*

The table or lectern doesn't care your audience cares! Get those eyes up and on them!

---

- **If you care about what you are saying so will those listening to you.**

- **If you keep your eyes on your listeners you will see if they are getting your message.**

- **If you fail to prepare you prepare to fail!**

---

Everything you say - everything you demonstrate will be geared to your purpose.

## At the end of my talk I want my listener to do.....

- You will talk **TO** and **AT** listener with eye contact
- In words they can easily understand
- In a vocal manner that makes it easy for them to listen and to easily pick up pertinent points
- You will spend as much time practicing as you do reparing - or more!!!

## Making Presentations Powerful

A Powerful Presentation Is One That:

- Shows audience you are prepared
- Starts with a "Road Map"
- Follows map with objective always motivating
- Is organized, complete, concise
- Reveals presenter as efficient, effective, easy to understand
- That replaces "I" with "YOU"
- Always ties presentation to benefits for listener

## Some Initial Questions To Ask:

1. Know why.  What do you want to happen?
2. What do you have to do/say to make it happen?
3. What do you need to have to help make it happen?
4. Who is the audience?
   What is the best way to get them to do what you want?

# Delivering a Presentation

● **Organizing Talk**

Why speaking? (What do you want audience to Do/ Know?) Who speaking to? (How much do they know already? etc.) What points do you want to make? Logical order for effect?

Jot down ideas in a free-wheeling manner. Leave spaces between words then cut in strips. Organize ideas in groups/add and subtract. (cut and paste or move on computer) Work on body first; then conclusion; **THEN** introduction.

● **Introduction**

Let's people know where they are going....listeners do not like mystery trips! Where going and how long! Avoid a **LONG** introduction. Build common ground quickly. Your first fifteen or twenty words are more important than your next fifteen thousand!

● **Body**

Keep logical. Use transitions to tie talk together. Keep a balance - don't use five minutes for one point and a minute and a half for next.

● **Conclusion**

Use to re-enforce; call for action; tell audience where you want them to go from here. Use quotation/poem/ statement etc.  If it drives point home.

## ● Do NOT try to memorize your talk

Develop a "Road Map" to move you from idea to idea. (Words or phrases to jog memory.) If you use a full text, treat it as a script. Double or triple spaced. Do not break up phrases at the end of a line. This will happen if you use **JUSTIFIED** typing for script.

Remember : *New idea - new page.* Use upper half or two thirds of page only.

Use **ORATOR** or Upper Case for ease in reading. Mark script (in pencil) for pauses; emphasis etc. PRACTICE reading aloud so eyes are UP when speaking. **KEEP PHRASES SHORT - TALK WRITING.** Be careful trying to "Wing it". Usually you will go too long or leave out important data.

## ● PRACTICE and TIME yourself

If you are overtime you may not have a chance to deliver your conclusion!

To calculate the **MINIMUM** amount of time you spend preparing multiply the time you will take by the number of people you will be talking to.

That is the time your audience is investing in you. Be worthy of this investment.

Another measure used by successful speakers: One hour of research and preparation for every minute you will be speaking!

- **If you are speaking in an unfamiliar space CHECK IT OUT ahead of time.**

  You may want to use a flip chart and the room is too long for that etc.

- **If you are using audio-visual equipment CHECK IT OUT before the audience assembles.**

  Be sure the microphone is working/how it works. Do you have to turn it on?

- **If you want questions afterwards be sure you have "primed the pump".**

  Set a couple of starter questions etc.

You will stand up and/or approach lectern or speaking space with confidence -**YOU ARE PREPARED.**

If you are being introduced, prepare an introduction and give to chair person ahead of time. This way you know the information will be correct; the content short and pointed to give the proper *'send off'*.

As you reach lectern or speaker's *'space'* make contact with the introducer (if this is an occasion calling for one). You do not have to give a public thank you. This can take away from your prepared introduction.

- **Do not GLANCE at notes before you SPEAK !!!!**

  Look over the crowd; pause; concentrate on your message and your audience. You look at your notes at the end of an idea only...your audience can digest that part of your message as you check on next point.

The best way to ensure success is **PRACTICE - PRACTICE - PRACTICE.**

## Cooper Communicating Tool

Remember the basic rules for effective presentations:

- **Stand up to be seen.**
- **Speak up to be heard.**
- **Sit down, as soon as your point is made, to be appreciated.**

# TAKING
# IT ONE
# MORE STEP
# TO SUCCESS

CONCLUSION

This chapter contains a few more examples of how to effectively professionalize your presentations through the use of visual aids and question periods. Practice in any of the keys or steps is the most important way to improve your speaking performance. **POW ! - R SPEAKING** can be learned if you follow the guides and communication tools in this book.

# Using Visual Aids

We learn through our **FIVE SENSES.** Your words have to create pictures.

## VISUAL AIDS:

- Clarify the picture. Re-enforce.
- Can cut across language barriers.
- Can be fun. Add variety to difficult presentation material.
- Make your presentation look more organized.
- Can explain complicated ideas more clearly.
- Take the focus off speaker.
- Give speaker "sign posts" to keep focused.
- Are often reusable.

## GUIDELINES:

1. **Remember visual will dominate.**
2. **Which form? Chart, slide, chalk board, video, flip chart?**
3. **Make sure they are visible.**
4. **Control the amount of information on each visual.**
5. **Don't use visual as your script.**

# Working with Visuals

To use your visual aids successfully you have to direct your audience.

- Don't let the equipment put you in second place. You are the Primary source of information

- Don't point at the screen if you can avoid it. Use pointer or pen on overhead.

- As soon as a picture is up on the screen people are going to read it!

- Your job is to make them read it your way. Here is a routine you can use: Let them see the full picture (count silently to 3 if you want)

- Then quickly satisfy their curiosity: They are thinking, "What is this slide telling me? " If you don't quickly Clear up the reason why - your audience will focus on their interpretation!

- Take their eyes where you want them to go Examples: "Here is a flow chart - You can see on the left side....." "Here are the three areas we need to concentrate on - the first bullet...."

- Do not just read the words they can see. You need to expand on them.

- You do not use your slides as your script!

- Remember - pictures often give more impact that words.

- If your overhead is introducing a section of your talk, keep remarks about it to a minimum. Your following slides can help you with details, comparisons, etc.

- Try to mix up the types of slides you use. Graphs, maps, bullets, pictures, one word slides, etc

# Visual Aids - Choosing Your Options

**Selection will depend on:**

- Size of audience
- Atmosphere of meeting
- How much time and money you can afford
- Convenience of handling

## FILM OR VIDEO:

- when interaction not needed
- you need/want to stage a scene to send message
- benefit to audience to see action sequence

## SLIDES:

- good for a large audience
- when you need photographic exactness
- you want to show many visuals in succession
- will use many times
- when you have lead time to create

## FLIP CHARTS

- for audiences up to 30
- good for recording audience input (often need two)
- can prepare ahead
- not too expensive

### OVERHEADS:

- when you want random access to visuals
- relatively inexpensive
- can be creative as slides
- can still see speaker
- can create quickly if needed
- can put notes on borders

### CHALK OR WHITE BOARD:

- inexpensive
- can be creative

# Handling the 'QUESTION PERIOD'

Many presenters want or need a question/answer portion as part of their talk.

### ADVANTAGES:

- You can clarify items.
- Re-enforce important points.
- Interact with the listeners.

### DISADVANTAGES:

- You lose a certain amount of control.
- Working under pressure - can disrupt clear thinking .
- You can blow the credibility established with carefully constructed speech.

- Comments from audience can cause a domino effect.
- Side issues can interfere with your message.

## How to structure questions to your advantage

### TIMING:

- Best at the end
- Gives you a chance to go through whole presentation first

## How to set up so your listener(s) will wait

- Ask them.  And give them a reason for the wait.
- Tell them how long you will take.
  How much time there will be for them.

### EXCEPTIONS:

- listener needs to / wants to ask questions to sure points are clear
- material complex - may need further information

# Some Methods for Controlling Your 'QUESTIONS PERIOD'

**Step 1:**   Raise your hand as you ask "Any Questions?"

**Step 2:**   You select questioner.

**Step 3:**   Really look at questioner and listen for issue behind questions.

**Step 4:** Break eye contact afterwards.

**Step 5:** Restate or rephrase.

**Step 6:** Look back at questioner and answer.

**Step 7:** End / don't end answer looking at questioner.

**Step 8:** Raise hand for next question.

# Remember in Questions and Answers You Focus on the Issue!

Questions are the words that hold together the issue. You must unwrap the package. You address the *'issue'* when you rephrase the question.

## Major Issues:

| | | |
|---|---|---|
| 1. | **Ability** | Do you have the talents to go it? |
| 2. | **Authority** | Are you allowed? |
| 3. | **Alternatives** | Is there another way? |
| 4. | **Priority** | Why not do this next? |
| 5. | **People** | Who will do it? |
| 6. | **Quality** | Are you able to do it right? |
| 7. | **Quantity** | How much will you do? |
| 8. | **Price Tag** | Is it affordable? |
| 9. | **Motivation** | Why are you doing it? |
| 10. | **Achievable** | Can you do it? |
| 11. | **Time Factor** | When will you do it? |
| 12. | **Method** | How will you do it? |

**Don't say "The Question is . . . .**          **PLUS:**

**Use the five W's and the H**

| | | |
|---|---|---|
| **What** | - will the restructuring do . . . | How often |
| **Why** | - begin with the junior staff . . . | Are we |
| **When** | - will this survey . . . | Did we |
| **Where** | - do you see this going . . . | Would I |
| **Who** | - is assigned . . . | Should you |
| **How** | - can you inspire . . . | Is this |

# Some Final Points to Get You on the Journey

## 1. Notes or not?

Use notes or a whole script if you need to! The point is to use them properly. You have the tools in this book to lift your words off the page and share your ideas.

**Reminder:**

**Do not read! Mouth open - eyes up!!**

Do not let your slides or overheads replace your notes! They are to help your listeners not to let you say "I never use notes. I have my slides." **WHAT'S THE DIFFERENCE?**

If you need notes or a script make sure the printing is **LARGE** enough for you to see. If you wear reading glasses you might want to make your notes when you are not wearing them. I do. I often misplace my glasses. This way I know I can always read the **LARGE** printing!

Keeps the sentences short! Talk write. This will make it easier for listeners to understand you.

## 2. Microphone or not?

●   **If there is one there - use it!**

Presume someone who has spoken in that room knows it is needed.

Watch the placement of your mike. It isn't a lollipop so don't feel you have to have it within an inch of your face! The best way to work with a microphone when you are talking is to position it about eight inches from your mouth and lower than you chin. To keep it from picking up all your mouth and breath sounds you are better to have it at an angle.

Do not lean over to a mike. Pull it up to you.

If you have a cordless mike **REMEMBER** it has an on/off switch. Turn it on before you speak. Make sure you turn it **OFF** after! And don't speak until you do.

## 3. Lectern or podem or not?

If it is there don't be afraid to use it. For your notes! Do not grasp the sides as if you were steering a snowmobile. Don't use it as a handy leaning post.

Feel free to move away from it if there is room to do so. If you need to do so, check the room beforehand to make sure there is space to do this.

## 4. How do you group your audience?

As close to you as possible. If you are in a long narrow room try to have the chairs facing a long wall. Leave space so you can move back and forth.

If you are using tables make sure they are positioned so everyone can see the speaker. Do not have too many chairs at each table. It means some people will have to move chairs or sit with their backs to speakers.

If you are speaking in a hotel conference room, check it out before hand. You will often find the chairs are too close together. Get them spaced apart. People do not listen well when they are crowded.

If you are using audio/visual equipment make sure it is positioned so that the equipment doesn't interfere with the sight lines of your audience.

# Some Last Words
# As you Prepare to
# Speak with Power

- **Put them where they will be reminders:**

  - Use the tools in this book and you will no longer be part of that 85% who fear getting up to speak.

  - If you care about what you are saying - so will those listening to you.

  - If you want a place in the sun be ready to put up with a few blisters.

  - If you fail to prepare you prepare to fail.

  - Even when you fall flat on your face you are still moving forward.

- Only the mediocre are always at their best!

- Think before you speak. You never have to explain something you haven't said.

- Remember WII-FM. Being right doesn't count unless the right people know you are right.

- The difference between ordinary and extraordinary is the **"extra"** you put in.

# GOOD LUCK

**BETTY K. COOPER**

Ms. Cooper also offers
In house Seminars, Workshops,
One-On-One Coaching
and Keynotes
on:


**Speak With Power**

**Powerful Professional Presentations**

**What To Say And How To Say It**


## Contact:

Cooper Communications
2209, 140 - 4 Avenue, S.W.
Calgary, Alberta
T2P 3N3
Telephone:    (403)   294-1313
Fax:             (403)   294-1315